The Life I Did *Not* Plan

*How My Life Turned Out Better
Than I Expected*

Sabrina Szabo

The Life I Did *Not* Plan: How My Life Turned Out Better Than I Expected. Copyright 2015 by Sabrina Szabo. All rights reserved. Printed in Canada. No parts of this book may be used or reproduced in any manner without written permission except in the case of brief quotations embodied in critical articles or reviews.

For information please email contact@brinaszabo.com
http://www.brinaszabo.com

Book and Cover design by Sabrina Szabo
Editor: Heather Conn

ISBN: 978-0-9949239-0-5

First Edition: December 2015

To my husband, Ferenc Szabo,

with all my love,

"Only Forever"

Acknowledgments

I thank God, the Father, and Jesus, the Son and the Holy Spirit, for all that I am, and for all that I have, as well as for His guidance in writing this book.

I would like to express my deepest thanks to my beloved parents, Jose Sergio and Maria Vaneilde, and to my husband's parents, Frank Sr. and Gabi, for their love, sacrifices, and support. I'm honoured to have you as my parents. I love you.

I also address my thanks to my two favourite people in the whole world: my sister Lili and my brother Marcelo. Don't ever doubt my love for you.

To my Brazilian family, especially my aunts Auxiliadora and Rita West, and to my Hungarian family: thank you for your support and encouragement.

My heartfelt gratitude to my editor, Heather Conn: thanks for your advice and corrections, and for editing my manuscript with love.

I wish to extend my utmost gratitude to Vania Aragao for never giving up on me and for showing me the light even when I didn't want to see. I will never forget your love and generosity.

Special thanks to all my friends in Brazil: Laura; Denise; Gardenia; Edna; Franklin; Murilo; Silvana; Almerindo; Carol; Janaina; Ariane; Elisa; Aldo and Helen. Special thanks, also, to my friends in Canada: Fabiana; Alexandre; Patricia; Delson; Alison; Mark; Chayene; Ben; Constance; Beth and Neal. People like you make this world a better place in which to live.

Finally, I thank my church family and my pastors for edifying, nurturing, and helping me to mature in Christ.

God bless you all.

The Life I Did *Not* Plan

Table of Contents

Chapter 1: I Shot Myself in the Foot.. 9

Chapter 2: Dumped, Broke, and Lonely Sinner 29

Chapter 3: Too Dark To See Much.. 47

Chapter 4: The Way It All Happened 56

Chapter 5: Avoiding Discomfort: Another Feeble Excuse For Fear.. 68

Chapter 6: Paid In Full: I Became Debt-free 79

Chapter 7: Best Friends For Life 92

Chapter 8: The Real Planner... 102

Chapter 9: We Speak English in Canada 112

Chapter 10: Antagonists: Every Good Story Has Them........ 124

Chapter 11: Canada Smells Like Coffee 136

Chapter 12: New Land, New Challenges, Same God............ 148

Chapter 13: They Need To Know and We Must Say It 160

Chapter 14: We All Have Skeletons in the Closet.................. 170

Chapter 15: The Dream Dress and a One-dollar Diamond Ring 178

Chapter 16: Fasten Your Seat Belts: The Elephant is Taking Off.. **187**

Chapter 17: Waiting in the Wings **196**

Chapter 18: Mi Casa, Su Casa, Jesus **204**

Chapter 19: Sales? No Sweat!... **214**

Chapter 20: Baptized in Clean, Cold Waters........................... **223**

Chapter 21: Bitter and Twisted.. **230**

Chapter 22: In God's Basket **241**

Chapter 23: Still Waiting, but Beating Some Odds **253**

Chapter 24: The Call of Duty **267**

Chapter 25: I Always Had My Head in a Book **277**

Chapter 26: A Letter From Me To You **289**

Chapter 1

I Shot Myself in the Foot

"For God did not call us to uncleanness, but in holiness. Therefore he who rejects this does not reject man, but God, who has also given us His Holy Spirit."

1 Thessalonians 4:7-8 (New King James Version)

LIKE MANY TEENAGERS, I grew up being bullied by my schoolmates. I was too skinny (believe me, it used to be a problem) and much taller than the other kids in my class. I also had to wear braces for my buck teeth. My mom never let me cut my hair, which was perfect: naturally light brown and sleek. It was so long, it used to cover my entire face. I could almost sit on it.

For many years, my fellow students at a private day school, five minutes away from our home in Brazil, picked on me because of my appearance. An even bigger reason was because I had one of the best grades in the entire school; that made a lot of them very jealous.

To provoke me, some of these kids came up with a bunch of awful nicknames. I only remember two of them, the ones that hurt me the most. "Toothpick" was definitely the most popular one; even the people who were nice to me would call me like that. The second one was "Scarecrow." Some really mean kids used to say that I looked so bad, I would never find a boyfriend; instead of attracting guys, I would probably scare them all away.

I learned soon enough that I had only two options to get rid of the bullies: confront them (and for that I had to be stronger or pretend that I was), or play their game (pretend that they were funny and laugh with them, even if I was the one they were making fun of). When bullies realize that you don't care, they usually leave you alone and look for other prey.

Well, I was too much of proud person to bow my head and cry over their hurtful jokes, at least not in front of them. So, I started to use both techniques. At age eight, I was able to stand up for myself and confront anyone; it didn't matter who the aggressor was. I lost count of how many times I got in trouble for being in a fight that I didn't start, and how many times my mother and I were invited to appear in the principal's office.

But that didn't mean I wasn't hurting inside. I wanted to be accepted, to be loved, and like any girl that age, I wanted to be popular.

At home it wasn't easy either. My mother, Maria, a typical, very feminine Brazilian woman, was tall and curvy (not fat) with long, dark-brown, wavy hair. She was raised to be tough, and losing her husband, my dad, when she was only twenty-eight had just made her even more stern and resentful. Her view was: "Only the strongest survive. We need to be strong and we need to be the best, no matter what." She used to say: "A 99.99 scale is not excellent, but it is very good. Only 100.00 is excellent." At the same time, she was deeply concerned that I would become more like my father's relatives: they were very proud and arrogant people. And sure enough, I followed their path.

For a teenager, it was a very difficult task to bridge these conflicting expectations and find a common ground: I always had to be first and the best, never second, in everything I did, and yet, I should never feel proud about it. Because this was too hard for me, my mom and I used to fight a lot.

She was always complaining that I could have done better, and yet, when I did excel, she would criticize and sometimes humiliate me in front of others, supposedly just to keep me humble. Despite my mother's good intentions, I grew up feeling ugly, unloved, unwanted, awkward, and not good enough.

Trying to fit in and to make people love me, I began to lie. I used to tell stories that didn't happen, just so the other teens around me would think I was cool. I would lie about all sorts of things. I created my own imaginary world, in which I not only had the same things as other people, but sometimes more and better things. For example, I said I had a pilot boyfriend who had his own helicopter; I travelled to the most exotic places and attended every concert in town. I lied so much that I even started to believe my own lies and never had a problem sustaining a story.

Then, one day, a guy I will call Tom showed up in my life. At first, I thought I would never need to lie again, that I could be myself with him. No more pretending or made-up stories. But I was wrong. Later on, I had to lie again, not once, but many times.

It was summer break in Brazil in November 1995. I was fourteen. Every year, all my cousins, my little sister Lili, and I would get together at my grandma's house, about half an hour away from my mother's home. It was a nice, old property that my grandfather, Sergio Francisco, a renowned engineer and architect, built for his family in downtown Aracaju. His three-storey, red-brick house had a large garden in front and a plaque bearing his name and position.

Nanny Raymunda used to love to have all her grandkids around, especially Lili and I; it was her only way to keep the memory of her son, our dad, alive. We always looked forward to that visit since grandma would never say no to us. At her house, we could do almost anything, and go anywhere we wanted. There, I spent the best days of my life—and the worse as well, but that will come later.

But back to Tom. He was a tall, skinny cyclist. His eyes were this warm caramel colour that I had never seen before. His hair was curly but he always kept it very short. He used to live in a building across the street from where my grandmother lived. He was my cousin Marta's best friend. They were both studying in their final year at the same school, getting ready to follow a new path at university.

When Marta needed to borrow a book from him, she asked me to go with her to his place to pick it up. As we arrived in front of the building, Tom was already downstairs. At first, we thought that he was waiting for us, but soon we realized that he was waiting for a woman he had met through one of those sex hotlines.

The woman arrived a few minutes after we did, wearing a low-cut T-shirt that read "Are you ready?" We could see her breasts popping out of it. She stayed there, watching Tom flirt with me, until Marta and I left. I know that this should have been the first sign of something truly wrong, but I was still a teenager, only fourteen and starting high school, while they were already adults; he was twenty-one and Marta, twenty. I had no idea what that woman was doing there; I thought she was just a friend of his, like Marta was.

The only thing I could think of was how Tom had looked at me. The circumstances didn't matter; someone had finally paid attention to me. Tom made me feel so special, I felt like I was beautiful and wanted. He was a playful man and his jokes and spontaneity attracted me. It was as if the huge gap in our ages and experience did not even exist. I couldn't sleep that night because I was thinking about him.

Tom, evidently, also kept thinking about me. The following day, he came to visit Marta and me at grandma's house. After that, he stopped by every day for the entire summer. That concerned my cousin since she saw my interest in him growing. She tried to open my eyes, letting me know that besides occasional dates with strangers,

Tom was dating two other girls simultaneously. She warned me: "You should not get involved with him."

I should have listened to her, but I couldn't—I was madly in love with him. When I confronted Tom about the other girls, he led me to believe that he had broken up with them because of his feelings for me. (Later, I learned that those girls broke up with him because they found out about each other and, consequently, who he really was.) He was my first boyfriend and I was ready to fight against the world to be by his side.

As the summer ended and school started, I had to go back to my mom's house. Because I was too young and my mom was very conservative, she did not, at first, approve of my relationship with my boyfriend. It was not so much because of our age difference, but mostly because it added stress and complications to her already demanding life. My mother felt a weight on her shoulders to prove to society that she was able to raise us well without a father.

When daddy passed way, mom was left alone with five-year-old me and Lili, about to turn two, to care for. Even though, some years later, she got married again, (that is how my little brother, Marcelo, entered our lives) she kept feeling that same pressure to prove to the world that she was, indeed, able to raise us well, despite having been a young widow and now, a remarried mother.

But Tom was highly skilled at creating a good first impression. He knew what to do to gain people's trust. So, after a long talk, we got my mother's blessings: we could see each other on Sundays afternoons, under her supervision. To get this agreement, I had to say "yes" to a lot of rules that she established. This ended up making our lives so miserable that it would have been better for Tom and I to go our separate ways rather than remain together.

Somehow, we made it work through the first year. I gave up on my early vacation with my cousins because my mom forbade me to go anywhere without her. I was never able to attend my friends' birthday parties and enjoy pleasures like going to a movie, to the beach or public pool. Even riding a bicycle without my mother watching me was prohibited.

The second year, when I was sixteen, was a bit more of a challenge. Tom broke up with me twice, both times because he found new girls who could go out with him; with them, he could get more intimate. That, obviously, made my mom furious and completely against our relationship. But I was blind and didn't see things from her perspective; the only thing I saw was that Tom was innocent. In my eyes, he only did what he did because of her rules.

With no more Sunday afternoons together or phone calls allowed during the week, the only option I had left was either to skip class to meet Tom somewhere far from school or skip my meals so I could arrive earlier at school and spend time with him at the nearby park, waiting for the bell to ring, indicating that class was about to start.

And I did both things, for several months. Because of that, I ended up sick in a hospital, for two weeks, with pneumonia.

Until then, I had only believed in God because I was taught that I should. I was baptized when I was a baby and had my first communion at age nine. After that, I don't remember going to church, or paying attention to anything related to God, but I do remember that I used to pray the same prayer every night before I slept. It was something like "Glory be to the Father, and to the Son, and to the Holy Spirit. As it was in the beginning, is now, and ever shall be, world without end. Amen." This was more of a habit than a belief.

Even though I tried to keep my distance from God or any religion, for some reason I always felt there was something else, something more that was I missing. I didn't know what or where to look. But in that hospital room, I started to think about all the people who had passed away, perhaps in that same bed (creepy, I know). I started to ask myself: "What happens to us after our lives come to an end?"

Coincidently, one of my mom's friends came to visit me and left me some books so I could kill some time and maybe stop thinking about what dead people had laid in my bed. But this didn't happen because the books were all about spiritualism, a belief based on the relationship between the spirits of living and dead people.

As I started to dig more into the subject of the afterlife, I thought I had found the answer I was looking for: karma. This explained the injustices that I had to go through, such as losing my father when I was still a child, and was an answer for the atrocities in the world. I shared with Tom what I had discovered from reading these books. He told me that his mother used to attend some meetings where a leader would speak on behalf of a superior entity, teaching things like how to achieve perfection as human beings, by reincarnation, throughout many lives. He promised to take me with them to one of these meetings once I was out of the hospital.

Well, that was what I was looking for. Since I wanted to be perfect, I thought I had it all figured out. I'd achieve perfection through karmic cleansing: by doing good deeds, mainly charitable giving. After leaving the hospital, I would be ready to start a more meaningful life, since I had found the missing piece of the puzzle. In addition, I was ready to have a grown-up conversation with my mom. I wanted to explain to her why she had found Tom beside me in the hospital more than once: we were back together. I was sure that if I knew how to use the right words, and after she saw how Tom took good care of me while I was sick, we would have her blessings once again, and we would no longer need to hide our relationship.

But things didn't go as well as I thought. While I was not at home, my mother went through my diary. Reading and digging through all my writings, she realized that I was no longer a little girl. She found out that I wasn't a virgin.

I had lost my virginity with Tom, at age fifteen, about a year before she found out. Even though I was a willing participant, I cried the day after at school when I looked at the other girls and imagined that I was the only one. I felt awkward and did regret it, but was raised not to cry over spilled milk, so I shook it off. With time, that didn't bother me anymore.

After I left the hospital, my mom waited a couple of days to talk to me about her findings. First, she wanted to make sure I was fully recovered from the illness. When I got stronger and ready to go back to school, she called me into her bedroom and gently asked me: "Will you and Tom get married?" I didn't understand the question. She didn't like him. Until then, Tom and I had fought hard so we could stay together. Suddenly, she tells me that she wanted us to get married? I thought that something was wrong with her.

She lied to me, saying that she was looking for a phone number in my diary when, by accident, she found out what Tom and I had done. But when I say she was lying, I truly mean it. There was no way for her to find that out just by looking at my diary, even more so, accidentally. I was sure of this because I never wrote anything about my feelings and experiences without using encryption. I created secret codes because she always had the habit of reading cards and letters that were either sent to me, or that I had written to someone.

Instead of screaming and yelling at me like she usually did, my mother was cold and spoke quietly, almost like she was whispering. Maybe she didn't want the neighbours to hear us. Lost in my thoughts about her odd behaviour, it took me some time to answer her.

"Are you and Tom planning to get married?" she asked me again.

Well, even a sixteen-year-old girl could know that getting married definitely wasn't the best solution. But I answered with what I thought she wanted to hear: "Yes, I guess. One day, maybe."

This wasn't exactly what she was expecting to hear. The tone of her voice changed drastically: she began to scream at me, but I didn't waver.

She knew me. She had trained me well enough to show no fear, not to surrender to any kind of circumstances. So she brought up a second option.

"You can pack up your belongings and move out," she said, seething. "Obviously, since you decided to have sex without my consent, you've proven that you're mature enough to either get married or live on your own." There wasn't a third option, so I took what I could with me and left for my grandma's house.

Tom and I couldn't get married, not at that age, not like that. Although I did love him, I wasn't sure he was the guy with whom I wanted to spend the rest of my life. Don't get me wrong; he was a good man and a very good friend—the only one I had.

That was one of the reasons why I didn't want to marry him. Every time that he broke up with me to be with other girls, Tom hurt me a lot. I was in love but I wasn't dumb. I knew no good could come from this relationship, but I always accepted him back because I had nobody else. My mom never allowed me to have friends; she always thought they were not good enough for me. After some time, even my cousins began to avoid me because my mother had insulted them numerous times.

Tom was the only person who wanted to be around me. I needed love and he was offering something that I thought was very much like it. But deep inside of me, I knew I deserved more.

My mother didn't like the option I picked. She thought she had control over the situation; so, when she gave me the second option, she didn't really mean it. She was just bluffing. She was expecting to scare me and make me change my mind.

She underestimated my ability to bear hardship.

But she was also a tough cookie and didn't settle for less than what she wanted. So, she began to terrify my grandma, telling her things like "Your son would have been so disappointed in you." She also made scenes in the middle of the street, arguing with everyone who opened their door to help me.

It was a horrible time in my life. I never felt so lost and undervalued. I had never cried in public before. Even when growing up, I used to lock myself in the bathroom and run the shower while I cried, so nobody could see or hear me. But these were different times. I cried for hours and hours, for weeks on end. It didn't matter where or who was with me. I remember that I went for a job interview and started to cry like a baby when they asked me why I wanted to work for them. Weeping, I told them my story and begged for help. That was how I got my first job.

It was in a shoe store at a new shopping mall about to open in our city. The salary was commission based and I had to pay for my own uniform. Every new season, we were asked to purchase a new set of clothing, so at the end of each month, what was left of my salary was mainly for food and transportation.

Tom saw that if he didn't help me, I would turn out to be a homeless, barely having enough to eat. He was a cashier at a local retail store that sold home improvement and construction products. He spent most of his salary on cyclist garments and bicycle tools and had never helped me financially before. Because he now felt responsible, he decided to follow my mother's wishes. At his twenty-third birthday party, he asked me to marry him in the presence of his family members. Although they put on fake smiles, their eyes couldn't hide how surprised and disappointed they were with the news. Still, we got hugs and wishes of happiness.

The night we got engaged, I had a dream. I was running after my brother Marcelo and sister Lili. My mom was there with them, pulling them away from me. They went inside a church to hide but I followed them. Halfway into the church, an invisible obstacle stopped me. I couldn't see what was it, but somehow, I could feel that it was the hand of a male angel. He began to tell me that if I went with him, he would show me a way out of this situation with my family. Although I was already conscious, my body wasn't responding to my command. I wanted to open my eyes and get up, but I couldn't. I started wrestling against the angel, who was pulling me up from the ground.

It all became so real that I could feel my soul leaving my body. I didn't know what was going on. I never believed in anything like angels, so I thought that death was taking me. And I didn't want to die. It was true that my life was a mess but I didn't think that dying was the best solution to my problems. I started to scream at the angel in the dream. "Leave me alone! I didn't want to go with you."

The dream had become a nightmare. After wrestling with it for a while, I woke up in tears. I didn't want to go back to sleep, so I spent the rest of the night awake. I was afraid that the angel would be waiting, again, to take me with him. When morning arrived, I felt overwhelmed. In my heart, I felt that I should not marry Tom.

 Yet, even though that foreboding and the memory of that dream kept bothering me night and day for weeks, I decided to marry him. I was afraid about my future. I was so confused and lonely. I didn't know what I would do living on my own at age of sixteen. So, a month later, Tom and I had our civil ceremony at city hall. That morning, a couple of hours before getting dressed, I thought of taking a cab and running away. But where could I go? Nothing came to my mind, so I put on my red gown (I chose red to represent my protest). By noon, we had signed the papers. I was a new bride.

 Since neither of us made enough money to start a life together, one of his relatives landed us a furnished apartment. Tom's mother provided most of our grocery shopping. But she had never wanted us to be together. Since the beginning, she used to say: "This union is not meant to be." After we got married, she began to count the months, expecting our relationship to end soon. She'd call us and say things like: "Wow, I'm surprised that you're still married." She would also always remind me that Tom only married me because my mom forced him to and that I was doing okay only thanks to their help.

Truth was: she never liked me or any other woman that Tom had dated. One time, during our first year of marriage, he and I used up all our savings to buy an old motorcycle to help us to get to work (we had kept our jobs: Tom in home hardware and me in shoes). The bike was so old that it would break down almost every day, in the middle of the street, and sometimes in dark and sketchy areas of the city. To keep Tom from getting into danger, his mother decided to sell our motorcycle and buy him a brand new one, without letting me know. I only found out the night he showed up at home, riding it. I was so hurt that they didn't involve me in the decision. But what hurt most was that he gave me back my part of the money from the sale of the old bike. He told me that his mother bought the new one in her name so that he would not need to sell it in case we got a divorce.

That was the first of many horrible aggressive fights that Tom and I had. He never hurt me physically, but was always punching doors, breaking objects, and threatening to go back to his mother's house and leave me alone.

In the apartment building where we lived, Tom and I were usually very harsh with a couple who lived in the unit above us. We didn't like them because of their religious beliefs and the way they would always talk about God and Jesus; they used to put cards with Bible verses under our door. But mostly, because they used to hear us fighting, they would try to help us reconcile, even though we never asked for their help.

For one entire year we didn't hear from my mom. She had cut all ties with me and didn't let me have any kind of contact with my siblings—until the day I had to call her.

A few days after our first wedding anniversary, Tom left me at Marta's door at 2 a.m. He told me: "I realized that I'm too young to be responsible for you. I don't want to be in a serious relationship while all of my friends, who are the same age, are travelling and enjoying life." So, I had no other option but to call my mother.

Chapter 2

Dumped, Broken, and Lonely Sinner

"Then it shall be, if you by any means forget the Lord your God, and follow other gods, and serve them and worship them, I testify against you this day that you shall surely perish."

Deuteronomy 8:19 (NKJV)

MY MOM DROVE ME TO THE SMALL, two-bedroom apartment where Tom and I had lived for the past year, so that I could pack my personal belongings. While driving me to my grandmother's house to drop me off, she drove in silence the entire way. I bet she was hurting, but that didn't keep her from pushing me away. Waving goodbye, she said: "I couldn't bear to live under the same roof with a divorced woman."

I couldn't believe what was happening to me. I knew my mother was against sex before marriage, so previously, I understood, somehow, when she didn't want to have me around. But this was totally different: to leave me on my own after the man she more or less forced me to marry had just dumped me was something else. I thought she was being unreasonable. It wasn't my fault. If we had not gotten married in the first place, I would not have had to carry the load of becoming divorced at age seventeen. But raised to be strong, I could not show any sign of weakness. I left the car and walked towards my new life as a divorced young woman.

Although absorbed in shame and pain, I had to deal with the situation all alone. To make things worse, a few months before Tom left me, I quit my job at the shoe store to dedicate my time to finishing high school and to study for the university entrance exam.

In Brazil, there are few tuition-free public universities. Therefore, these exams are highly competitive. Depending on which career path you want to follow, there are sometimes more than a hundred candidates per vacancy. Unfortunately, the public education system in Brazil still needs a lot of improvement. To get their children into a good university, but mostly to keep them in a safe environment, Brazilian parents usually spend a fortune with private schooling. My siblings and I have always studied in private schools.

Thankfully, my mother understood that I had a lot on my plate. I was heartbroken, had nobody to comfort me, no money to pay for my living expenses, and a lot of pressure to get into university. She also knew that it would be too hard on me to change to a public school halfway through the year, where the rules and environment were so different. So she promised that she would help me by paying for my last year at school.

But my mom made it clear that this would be the only help from her that I could count on. She wrote all the cheques with the exact amount of the monthly fee and the payee's (the school) name. This would ensure that only the school could bank the cheque, in case I thought about cashing the money and using it for any other purpose.

I thought I had reached rock bottom. Within only a year, I was kicked out of my mom's house, got married, then Tom abandoned me at my cousin's door. Now I had to live with my grandma, my aunt (dad's younger sister), her daughter (my cousin), and her son. Because I didn't have a job and couldn't contribute to household expenses, my aunt and her daughter frequently humiliated me. Like me, they were living off my grandma's income, which now had to be divided by five. Many were the fights we had over the amount or kind of food I was allowed to eat, the amount of water I spent having shower, or how much energy they could save if I didn't have the light on when studying in my bedroom.

One time, I sold my old bicycle to one of our neighbors, hoping to have some money for snacks and public transportation. It took me a while to receive the money. Because I thought he had forgotten to pay me, I decided to knock at his door and remind him of our deal. But then he told me he had trusted my aunt to deliver the money to me because I was not at home when he showed up to pay two days after I had sold the bicycle. Embarrassed, I went back home and confronted my aunt.

"The money belongs to me to pay for your stay," she yelled at me.

"But grandma never asked me to pay anything," I reminded her.

She wouldn't listen. Crying and nervous, my grandma begged us: "Stop yelling at each other." But my aunt kept going on and on with her insults and I did the same.

"You're a weight on everybody's shoulders, don't you see?"

"At least I'm not in my fifties still living with my mom," I replied.

When she realized that I would not back down, that I wasn't intimidated, my aunt changed her strategy and started targeting my parents. She said horrible things about them, such as "Your dad should have never married your mother in the first place" and "Having your sister and you was a huge mistake on their part." Which made me so angry that our fight almost got physical. I wanted to hurt her as much as I was hurt, but out of respect for her age (she was in her fifties); I turned around and locked myself in my bedroom.

    Besides, I knew that even if I had a chance to win that war, I would need to move out. After all, my aunt and her daughter were at my grandma's before I needed a place to live, and that was the only one I had. So, I managed to swallow my anger and pride. In the following months, I avoided more conflicts by keeping as much distance from them as I could. I would leave the house before they were awake and showed up at home only late at night, just before it was time to go to sleep.

    I would never have been able to do that if wasn't for the help of my best friend, a girl that I will call Kayla. We had met at school when I was still married to Tom. After he left me, she stepped out to help me as much as she could. Kayla invited me to her house every day, after class, where her mother and sisters fed me and offered me a quiet place to study until I had to go back home. Kayla never let me spend one day alone. She took me with her almost everywhere she had to go, like a mother with her newborn baby. She even took me to have dinner with her and her boyfriend, at his grandmother's house, who had never met me before that day, just so I would not have to go back home and starve until morning. We were always together. We had so much fun. I don't know what my life would be like today if weren't for her love and compassion.

At school, things were not going well. I was never on time because of the one-and-a-half-kilometre walk or because of the weather. The weather also didn't help. In Aracaju, during the summer, the heat is already unbearable at 7 a.m., which makes it too hard to walk fast. Even when I could get there on time, I was so tired and sweaty; I could barely pay attention to the teachers. My grades were just average. Most likely, I would not pass the university entrance exam. But I just didn't care about that anymore. The only thing I wanted was to finish high school and find a job that could pay for my rent and survival.

One day, after being sent home for the third time in the same week, I was called into the principal's office to have a talk. She was a very strict woman; students feared her so much, they avoided walking by her office. But to me, she was great. I admired how she imposed discipline with grace.

She wanted to know what was going on with me; she knew from my past that I was always a good student. I burst into tears and told her my story. After listening to what I said, that amazing woman offered me a deal: if I brought my grades back to "above average," she would give me a discount on my monthly fee. This way, I could use the change to pay for the bus ticket, and would never have to be sent home again, because of lateness. I took the offer and finished high school. I didn't pass the exam, but I did start a full-time job at a cosmetics and perfume store in downtown Aracaju.

My life was getting better. The store was a good place to work and I met some nice people. However, after being apart for almost six months, Tom persuaded me to start dating him again. At that time, the bank where my mom worked transferred her to a city far from Aracaju. Her house was empty and her parents had sold their farm in the country. They were finally retired and wanted to move to the city, so they decided to watch over my mom's house while they were looking for a place to buy.

They had heard about the things I had put with while living with my aunt and her daughter. Because they felt sorry for me, they invited me to move back to my mom's house and live with them. At last, I thought that my life was getting on track.

But nine months later, my mother was transferred back to town, so I had to leave her house again. Since I needed to find a place to rent, Tom decided that it was time to give our marriage a second chance. He asked me, "Can I move in with you?" I'll explain my answer and rationale in a minute.

Tom humiliated me a lot while we were "dating again." He felt embarrassed to tell his friends and family that we were back together, because this would have meant that he was wrong and acted irresponsibly to break up with me to enjoy life with his buddies. So, he kept our relationship a secret. Many times I had to hide myself behind doors, under the bed, or leave places in a hurry so no one could see us.

I said "yes" to Tom again. I wanted him to admit, publicly, that he regretted all the bad things he had done to me. Besides, after all those years we spent trying to make our relationship work, we ended up developing some true affection for each other.

So, even though I was aware that moving in together was far from the smartest thing to do, and that my reasons weren't right, I was happy to do so. I thought things could get better between us, and I really loved the idea of having a place that I could call mine, somewhere I could settle for a while.

Tom and I both started to work as representatives for a pharmaceutical company. These multinational laboratories pay a very good salary, even today. Tom had started to work in the field first. Then, because I helped him a lot, trying to impress doctors with good gifts and ideas, I got an interview at one of his employer's competitors. Subsequently, they hired me. We tried to keep our employers' competition out of our home life, but once in a while, we ended up fighting about work.

We rented a brand new, never-rented-before apartment for a good price, close to the university campus, where Tom was finishing his degree in public relations and marketing. I loved that we had a spare room where we could keep all the medication sample boxes that Tom and I received from our respective pharmaceutical companies.

Our life style changed for better. With our high income, we were able to buy land by the beach, fifteen minutes away from the city. Once it was paid for, we planned to build our own house. We hired engineers, architects, and a contractor to create a house the way I had always dreamed.

But one year later, Tom lost his job, which produced financial stress for us. We had used all the money we had saved to put a down payment on the lot. My salary alone wasn't enough to keep up with all our expenses.

That year, as my relationship with my mom got a little better, I felt I could ask her for help. She agreed to let us stay in her house and live with her until Tom could find work. Then we could rent a place again. Later on, she suggested that we should stay with her until our house was built and ready to move into.

Remember the fights I had with my aunt? They were nothing compared to the ones we had over the four years we spent living with my mom. There were fights between my mother and I, Tom and I, and my mother and Tom. And I just couldn't bear that any longer. I needed to do something, but didn't know what. Worse than that, I didn't know where else to find help.

I tried everything that I thought was worth a try. I started by regularly attending the Spiritualism Centre, thinking I could find an answer to my suffering. I wanted to understand why my mother was always so hard on me, why Tom was always threatening to leave me every time we had an argument. Why was I so unworthy of being loved? Besides that, I was never satisfied with my achievements. I always felt so empty inside. Nothing that I did or had would fill that hole in my Soul. I needed to find out what was wrong with me.

The answer I got at the Centre was that it had to do with my past-life karma: bad spirits lived in the body of good people. I ended up even more confused and also scared to death to know that the spirit of an enemy, from a previous life, could now be inside my mother's body. So I stopped going there.

Still trying to solve the problem, I took a holistic approach; I started with some reiki, then some crystals, and afterwards, read some Wicca books. Even though I didn't agree with reincarnation and spells, I thought that the Wiccan rituals and dances, the symbolic power of colours and their effects on human perceptions, and all that appreciation for life and nature were super cool. So, I decided to become one of them. And that's how I was introduced to the tarot and started visiting fortune-tellers.

I needed answers. I was twenty-four and had quit several companies; some of them were the best pharmaceuticals and medical diagnostics ones in the world. Within five years, I switched three university courses and ended up graduating in human resources management, which I never got to practice because I never worked in the field. Instead, I continued as a pharmaceutical representative, bought a fancy car and fashionable clothes and was having a house built by the beach. Before going to work, I was paying a professional to teach me how to surf in the mornings and I had a personal trainer waiting for me at the gym in the afternoon, after work, to help me with my workout. I was young, smart, and successful, and became a very attractive woman. Yet, I was deeply unsatisfied. The tarot reader didn't give me any answers but she did say something that changed my life drastically. She told me that someone from Tom's family would die. She even said it would be one of his uncles, and that his death would affect us deeply. After she was done, I ran away from there and didn't say a word about my visit to her studio to anyone. I promised myself that I would never go back there again for any reason.

    I tried to forget that prediction but one of Tom's uncles *did* die, many months later. He was fighting depression, and the disease won the battle—he ended his life. It was tragic and painful for all who knew him Nobody could have imagined this; even I, knowing what I knew, could not have thought of something like that.

    However, every now and then, I would remember what that woman said and guilt would consume me. The pain of knowing that something so bad could happen and not knowing when, to whom, and how was unbearable. As I realized that humans were not meant to know the future, I gave up on Wicca, holistic things, the horoscope, and tarot.

After going through all these frustrating experiences, I finally understood what was going on with me. I didn't need a bunch of rules and rituals. I did not even need answers anymore. I was tired of having taken care of myself since I was sixteen, of trying to impress others and fit in. Mostly, I was done begging for love.

What I needed was a saviour, someone who could take me away from the mess I was in and give me hope for a better future. So, I secretly decided to get divorced.

I had to be single again to meet "the one," the man who would erase my past, fill in the blanks of my life, and write, with me, a happy ending to my love story. With him, and only with him, would I feel that I belonged to a family. But I couldn't just go home and say that to Tom, not without starting a new war against my mother.

Strategically, I quit my job at a private bank and started to work in a city two hours away for a bank controlled by the Brazilian government. I needed guaranteed permanent employment, offered to every federal government employee in the country. Knowing my family, I knew they would not approve of my decision.

Once my marriage was over, so would be my relationship with them. I had to make sure I would never need to ask for help again.

But nine months after I started working there I was still married—because I didn't have enough courage to confront my mom.

The house that Tom and I were building was almost ready and I felt pressured to do something before it was too late. So, I suggested that we should get married at church.

Yes, I did say that. You didn't read it wrong.

I always dreamed of the day when I would marry the man I chose, wear a white dress, walk down the aisle, have a party for both of our families, dance our first song as Mr. and Mrs., and go for a trip on our honeymoon. Somehow, in my craziness, I thought that if I allowed Tom to be my chosen one, if we could start all over again, and be how it was supposed to have been in the beginning, maybe I would learn to love him and then the divorce wouldn't be necessary.

Although we were both baptized as babies at the same Catholic church near by grandmother's house, we hadn't been in a church since. Nevertheless, we decided to have the ceremony there.

However, about a month before the big day, I regained my senses and realized how bad this idea truly was: because I was afraid of living alone, I would trade vows with someone I never really loved. So, one day, while we were driving on a busy highway with Tom at the wheel, I told him: "I think we should wait a little more with the wedding. I'm not so sure that is the right thing for us to do now."

A very proud person, he didn't take the news as well as I had expected. He let go of the steering wheel. Facing me, he punched the windshield and yelled: "There's no way I'm going to let you embarrass me like that!" He was more concerned about how he would face his friends and family than anything else I had just told him.

Because he was acting so aggressively, I felt truly scared. I kept asking him to look back at the road, to grab the wheel of his sporty silver Chevrolet hatchback, which he loved more than anything in the world, and not kill us both.

"Will you agree to leave things the way they are?" he hollered as the vehicle careened sideways. Although raised not to fear anyone, I was terrified. Tom was driving at least a hundred kilometres an hour with no hands on the wheel and no eyes on the road.

"Y-y-y-yes," I stammered eager to calm him down.

"That's more like it," said Tom. Reassured, he returned his focus to driving. The night before the wedding ceremony, we met with the priest. He wanted to know more about our relationship and why we had decided to get married. I told him a lie, creating a story I thought he would like to hear.

"We want to start a new season in our lives," I said, "and we need God's blessings."

"Would you like to confess?" the priest asked at the end of our meeting.

"No!" I said immediately. Thankfully, Tom didn't want to either.

Even though I wasn't religious, I knew that I was living in sin. If I told the priest the truth, he would refuse to do our wedding. That would embarrass not only Tom, but both of our families.

The next morning, I walked the aisle, wearing a beautiful and charming white dress, carefully handpicked, to cover my dark soul. But don't get me wrong. I enjoyed the whole dressing-up-and-taking-pictures thing. About seventy of our friends and family were gathered together. Right after the party, Tom and I travelled to a nice cabin on a heavenly beach almost three hundred kilometres away: the perfect place for a honeymoon. Since we had never taken time to travel before that, in the midst of that fake happy moment, I thought our relationship could get better. It was like that saying, "Fake it till you make it."

But, despite all our efforts, it didn't work. Three months later, after a therapy session, I left the psychologist's office and invited Tom to a restaurant. Finally, I had the courage to end our miserable life together.

As expected, my mother showed me the door as soon as we told her what was going on. I had still held a small hope that she would let me stay with her for at least a week or so, until I found a place to rent. But she didn't. And once again, I was out on the streets without knowing where to go. This time, it was in the middle of the night.

I tried to get help from a very good friend but her husband didn't want me around. He was afraid that I could influence her to do the same and divorce him as they were always fighting and hurting themselves

"I'm so sorry, Sabrina," she said, half-asleep in her pyjamas with the door half open and her husband glaring at me behind her. "I can't.". Crying like a baby, she closed her door. I left her house, also in tears.

Chapter 3

Too Dark To See Much

"But when I looked for good, evil came to me; And when I waited for light, then came darkness."

Job 30:26 (NKJV)

IN THE MIDDLE OF THE NIGHT, driving my car and thinking of going to a hotel, I had a different idea suddenly pop into my head. *I should call Tina.* We had known each other for a little more than six months, were not close friends, but for some reason, I felt like I should call her. It was late. Tina and her mother were probably sleeping. But her mother answered the phone, opened their door, and gave me a place to sleep—not just for that night, but for many others. They gave me a spare key to their house so I could get in and out any time I needed, until I found an apartment to rent.

They were so nice to me. They heard my story, and even though what I had done was clearly wrong, they didn't judge me. I'm not saying that they approved of what I did, but the way they accepted me and included me in their lives, I felt like I belonged to their family, that we were all brothers and sisters. And I really enjoyed that. Through their unconditional love and compassion, they were truly special people.

I asked them why they were so accepting and if they always acted like that with strangers. I was curious. But, I have to admit, I was expecting a different answer. They started telling me about each of their past mistakes and how they were forgiven and free from condemnation because of the sacrifice of Jesus on the cross.

"Sabrina, we all make mistakes," Tina said. I shook my head in agreement. She continued: "But to live in condemnation is to deny the love of God for His people. When He sent Jesus to this world, His only Son, it was so He could redeem us all."

I never really believed in that Jesus thing. I always thought He was just another saint that the Catholic church created to rule uneducated people. But I agreed to go to Mass with them the following Sunday. I was still curious to find out what made this family so special. Why did they treat me so well when I least deserved it?

During the ten days I stayed with them, we went one more time to the church. Although we talked a lot about God, the Bible, love, and forgiveness, neither those conversations nor what I had experienced in our relationship were enough to break my rocky heart. There were a lot of changes I was not willing to make in my lifestyle to become one of these Jesus followers, such as pray and read the Bible every day, or go to church every Sunday and give money to them. So, as soon as I found an apartment, I went back to being the old me and left that entire faith thing behind.

Yet, living by myself for the first time at age twenty-four started to scare me deeply. I had terrible nights whereby I would not sleep; I was afraid of not waking up and being found dead many days later.

I didn't want to unpack my belongings because that would make me face reality. That was also too scary.

Once again, I knew what I had to do, but didn't know how to start. Or perhaps, I didn't want to start. Tom was the only person I knew who could help me. He was always the easy and practical solution; besides, I had no record of my adult life without him. So, one day, in the midst of my conflicting emotions, I told him I wanted my horrible but comfortable life back. I asked him to help me get settled and invited him to come to the apartment. I thought we could try one more time.

But after suffering the public humiliation of being sent back to his mother's house three months after our wedding party, he wouldn't, of course, just come back to me, not without making me pay for what I had done to him. To make things worse, his mother, who never wanted us together anyway, began to make up stories about me. She said that I insulted her many times and started to poison Tom's mind, bringing up the worse about me: all my mistakes, faults, and imperfections. She wanted to make sure that her son and I would never be a couple again.

And she did a pretty good job. Tom not only believed her lies, he started to call all our family members and friends, doing the same thing: telling horrible stories about me to put them against me and to gain their compassion. He was hurt and needed to know that people were feeling sorry for him. It was super easy to convince everybody that I was a wolf in sheep's clothing.

After all I had to endure; I have to tell you that I turned out to be a very sour person. Arrogant and rude many times, I knew I was very smart for my age. I had money, prestige, and was a very beautiful woman. My pride became my shield and seduction my weapon. To protect myself from being hurt again, I humiliated a lot of people.

Besides Tina's family, I could count on one hand who stood by my side. One of them was a single girl I will call Sara. She was also twenty-four and used to living her life like there was no tomorrow. Trying to help me get back on my feet, she did what she knew best: she invited me to parties, clubs, games, and movie nights. She introduced me to all her friends and to her sister, who I learned later, used to read tarot cards.

I broke the promise to myself not to consult them anymore and asked her to read them for me. Since I was a control freak, not knowing what would come next was hurting me more than all the payback that Tom was putting me through. I don't remember much of what she said, plus I thought she was just pretending to know how to read, so I didn't give her much credit. But that encouraged me to look for a professional tarot reader.

I knew a lady who used to live very close to my mother's house and decided to knock at her door. Her niece, whom I will call Brenda, answered the door. She told me her aunt no longer lived there but that she, too, was able to read the tarot. She offered to give me a reading. After I told her about my situation, she began to share her own story. She was once married to a policeman who used to abuse her verbal and physically. Because of that, she had to leave home and went back to live with her parents with a five-year-old daughter.

Although Brenda was a teacher, she was on a leave of absence because her husband had threatened to take her life the last time they had a fight. Since she couldn't go back to work, she became depressed. She found that reading books was a way to keep her mind busy; it helped her avoid destructive thoughts. Because I was also getting depressed, she recommended that I do the same.

Brenda believed in God and angels, good ones and bad ones, so she recommended that I pray, all day, every day, to keep the bad ones far from me. That was all I could remember from our talk.

A couple of days later, I was celebrating Christmas Eve with her and her family. (My mother always held a family gathering in her house; I thought she would need some help with the decorations, so I had arrived a few hours before the party. To my surprise, as soon as I got there, she asked me to leave, as fast as I could, before the other family members arrived. According to her, having me there would cause her a lot of embarrassment.) Crying so much after that, it was hard to keep my eyes open. I had left my mom's place, heartbroken. My tears almost blinded me as I walked along the empty streets, disoriented. Everyone else was indoors, celebrating with their family and friends.

I had found myself at Brenda's door. Her family invited me in and offered me food. While I was there, the neighbour next door kept playing the same gospel song over and over. It was so loud I couldn't help but pay attention to the lyrics. In Portuguese, they reinforced that Christ will be with you during dark times and that He wants you to be happy.

For days, I couldn't get that song out of my head. Unconsciously, I kept repeating its chorus in my mind. It was so annoying that I decided to look up the lyrics on the Internet and check how the rest of the song went.

I just read the entire song once, and those words stuck in my heart.

After that, I decided to give Jesus a chance to convince me of his existence. So I began to recite, very often, the same prayer I had learned as a little girl. It was something like *I believe in Jesus. I believe he died for our sins and was raised from the dead.* I also started attending the same Catholic church where Tina's family took me when I was with them.

But after a few weeks of doing the same thing, I didn't feel or see anything different, not in my life, nor in my heart. In fact, my life turned out even worse than before. Tom became more aggressive and started to send me horrible emails and text messages. Sometimes I would answer his phone calls and he would insult me for hours. I was deeply depressed and not eating well. I was just skin and bones.

Close to losing my mind, I decided to buy a book; I was trying to do what Brenda recommended. I went to a bookstore, hoping to find some good escapist fantasy to keep my mind busy, away from my dismal reality.

I did find a good book in the self-help section; its rough English translation would be *Seven Steps for a Better Life*. The author wrote it to help people like me, who were lost, to find their path to a better life. But that wasn't why I chose to buy it. Until that day, I felt convinced that there wasn't just one way to happiness. After all, we live in a world filled with all kinds of people and a huge diversity of cultures. To me, it seemed like he was saying that symbolically, there was only one medication for all kinds of diseases. I thought he was a fraud. So, I dared myself to read the book, apply those steps, and write him a letter, proving that he was misleading people and using their pain to make money.

Chapter 4

The Way It All Happened

"Nevertheless the solid foundation of God stands, having this seal: 'The Lord knows those who are His,' and, 'Let everyone who names the name of Christ depart from iniquity.'"

2 Timothy 2:19 (NKJV)

THAT BOOK I BOUGHT had a Bible reference for all sorts of situations that we may or may not face. I have to admit: it surprised me. I thought the author was giving his own interpretation of the Bible verses just to make a point, to have a kind of "Jesus signature" in every story that he narrated. I couldn't believe that a book written thirty-five hundred years ago could be so up to date. So, I borrowed a Bible from a colleague known for being a believer. My initial idea was to find in the Bible the same verses from the book I bought, to see if they were, indeed, there, and, if they held the same meaning in their original form.

And that was how I fell in love with Jesus: reading the Scriptures.

I started to read the *Seven Steps* book with more enthusiasm and kept my borrowed Bible for longer than I first had planned. To every chapter, there was a new verse. The more I dug into the Bible, the more I began to see the difference between the God I heard about and the God that I started to love.

I had a hunger to know more from the Bible that I couldn't explain. Little by little, those words started to change me and I began to behave differently. I printed out my favourite verses and stuck them all over my doors, bathroom mirror, and my computer at work. I would spend my lunch time at church (there was a Catholic church beside the branch where I used to work) or having long conversations with other believers about the things I was learning. I bought my first Bible and spent most of my weekends reading from it, sometimes sitting on the floor in my bedroom for hours. I had the Scriptures and pen and paper always available. From time to time, I would catch myself trying to find verses for everything that would happen to me during the day. Frequently, I would quote some of those verses when someone I knew had to face similar situations.

I started to feel the urge to visit my old neighbour, Vania, from the first place I lived in when I was sixteen and newly married. She was the one I didn't like because she was always talking about Jesus and salvation. But I didn't pay much attention to that feeling, even though it came to me again and again.

I was too proud to show up at her door, seven years later, and tell her that I wanted to know more about Jesus. I also knew she would ask me about Tom and I would have to tell her what happened to us. I wasn't ready to confess my mistakes and to share the humiliation. Besides, I had learned, from studying the Bible, God's word about divorce. It didn't matter how hard I tried, I couldn't change the fact that I never really loved Tom, and that he was already in another relationship, happier than he could ever be. I was immersed in shame and thinking the worst about myself. As much as I read about forgiveness and mercy, I still couldn't believe that I was worthy of any. I was basically pouring new wine into an old bottle:

No one puts a piece of unshrunk cloth on an old garment; for the patch pulls away from the garment, and the tear is made worse. Nor do they put new wine into old wineskins, or else the wineskins break, the wine is spilled, and the wineskins are ruined.

But they put new wine into new wineskins, and both are preserved (Matthew 9:16-18 NKJV).

Yet, I kept reading the Bible and tried to follow some of the simple steps the author mentioned in the book I bought. I started making small changes in my daily routine. Then, many things that I used to think were okay to do, suddenly became wrong. Things like not trusting in fortune-tellers, not worshipping any other God; Wicca is a religion that venerates the Sun, the Earth and the Moon, I also used to worship beauty, money and status. I never used drugs or smoked cigarettes but I did get drunk a few times. I used to lie a lot, mistreated a huge number of people with my intolerance, and after I heard that Tom was in a serious relationship, had a lot of boyfriends.

I decided to get rid of my old Wicca books; in doing so, I found a little card in the shape of a heart, handmade and written by Vania. She had given it to me for my seventeenth birthday, saying that she loved me and that Jesus loved me as well.

It was too much of a coincidence, I thought. Deep inside, I knew it was a sign that I should go to her house and talk to her. But I rejected the idea of opening up to a stranger, so I put the card in the garbage with all the other stuff.

A week after that, I was sitting at church, waiting for the Mass to begin, when Vania's older daughter sat down beside me. I choked. I couldn't believe what was happening to me. I couldn't pretend that I didn't see her—she was right beside me. Nor could I pretend that I didn't recognize her because she looked exactly the same since the last time we met. So, when the sermon ended, we talked a little and I asked her, politely, about her family.

"Guess what?" she replied. "My mom is waiting outside. Why don't you come out and say 'Hi'?"

She wouldn't take no for an answer. She was so persistent, I agreed.

"Just to say 'Hi'," I said.

But I said a lot more than that. For almost two hours, I told Vania my whole story. And just as I had imagined it would happen, I confessed my mistakes and shared the things I had been learning by reading the Bible.

To my surprise, Vania had a very similar story of her own. To surprise me even more, the first thing she recommended was to look for a hairdresser, to fix my hair colour. Truth is, I really needed to touch up my roots; they were about five inches long. The reason why I had stopped dying my hair was the same reason why I stopped going for a manicure or pedicure and began to wear large, ugly clothes: I was trying to get rid of my pride. I thought that was the way to start.

"You've got it all wrong," Vania told me. "You're like the Pharisees who missed the opportunity to become closer to God, even though they knew His Word very well, because their hard hearts couldn't accept that God hates the sin and not the sinner."

I had this wrong idea that first, I needed to be good enough. Only then could I belong to a family. I had kept focusing on what I should do, instead of focusing on what He had already done, through Jesus, on the cross. I was wasting my time, trying, all alone, to fix things at a surface level and setting myself up for failure, when the Creator of the Universe was asking me to let Him fix, once and for all, what was wrong in my inner being.

Vania invited me to show up on Monday night at church, where she led a prayer meeting, part of a movement called Catholic Charismatic Renewal, a movement within the Catholic church. I attended and the meetings were great. We would worship the Lord, singing and dancing beautiful songs. Afterwards, Vania used to preach to us. Some people from the group would pray for those in need. At the end, there was always someone giving testimony of healing and miracles that either took place right there, or later on in their lives. Many people, including me, said that they felt the presence of the Holy Spirit during the meetings.

As I started to dive into the Christian faith, I learned about the presence of the Holy Spirit and how God talks to us through Him. They used to say they heard a still, small voice coming from their Soul, guiding them to do what God's desire was for them. Or they would answer questions, giving comfort, wisdom, and peace. I wanted to be part of that; I was desperate to hear His voice. I started to pray every day, asking God to talk to me. I knew He was there with me but I wanted to feel it.

One early morning, around 3:20, I felt like I was being called. Alone at home, I didn't hear any noise but had the unique sensation that someone was calling my name. Terrified, still in bed, with my eyes closed, I began to pray. It was the first honest conversation I had with God; I brought up all my worries and fears, one by one.

I didn't know what to do with the house that Tom and I were building. I repented that I didn't pay attention to Vania when I was still young and she was trying to save my marriage. But I just couldn't repent my divorce. I couldn't picture myself spending the rest of my life with someone that I should have never married. At the same time, I didn't like that I was living completely alone either.

Although I never wanted to have children with Tom, I still had the dream of one day having my own family.

I questioned Him about why I was never satisfied with anything I had accomplished. I was known as a person who always started things but never finished them because I would lose interest halfway through. I went on and on about my problems with my mother, my work, and financial situation. After the divorce, my debts were too high and I thought I would never be able to pay them all off.

When I finished my prayer, it was already time to get up and shower to go to work. Previously, every morning, I would open the Bible randomly and read the first verse I would put my eyes on. After that, I would make notes and meditate on the verse throughout the day. So, like on any other day, I opened my Bible. But, this time, what I read brought me to tears. While I was reading these verses, my body was shivering. My heart rate accelerated dramatically—I could barely breathe. This is what I read:

"Behold, the days are coming," says the Lord, "that I will perform that good thing which I have promised to the house of Israel and to the house of Judah: In those days and at that time I will cause to grow up to David A Branch of righteousness; He shall execute judgment and righteousness in the earth. In those days Judah

will be saved, And Jerusalem will dwell safely. And this is the name by which she will be called: THE LORD OUR RIGHTEOUSNESS" (Jeremiah 33:14-16, NKJV).

In these verses, I found peace. They were the answer to my earlier prayer. Not one topic that I had addressed during my conversation with God was left out; there was a promise for each one of them. That was the first time I felt His presence. I was already a believer, based on what I learned about what He did for His people, but after this experience, my relationship with Him became personal.

As I surrendered myself completely, in the midst of fear, being honest and talking to Him as he was there, beside me, hearing me, Jesus came along and said, "Yes, I'm here with you. Yes, I can hear you" and "Yes, I am talking to you." I would love to tell you that from that day on, my life turned around, and all my problems were gone. But that would be a big fat lie.

A few weeks after my encounter with Jesus, the Carnival holiday arrived. Most people think that Carnival is a parade that happens once a year, in Rio de Janeiro, but the entire country stops for four days and parties go on in about every corner of every city. That year, I decided to spend the holiday attending a retreat called "Life in the Holy Spirit." People like me, who no longer wanted to be part of that world culture, would hear more about the love of God, his mercy, and how to live a life filled with His presence.

All went well, and I had a good time—until the last day.

It was Tuesday morning, the last day of Carnival. We had a workshop about forgiveness and I was still struggling with that. It was very difficult for me to forgive my mother for all that she made me go through; even more difficult was to forgive myself for all the things I did wrong in my life. So, I decided to take baby steps. To start, I was determined to visit my mom that same day, during our lunch break.

My mom was a little surprised, but glad to see me. Lunch was good. We didn't fight and that was really something to be grateful for. But because I didn't have much time, I had to leave soon after we ate; the last workshop was about to start and I didn't want to be late.

As I walked to the bus station on a deserted street, I saw a motorcycle coming in my direction. Two young men, both dressed in black, were riding it. I tried to turn around and walk as fast as I could, but didn't run, because I didn't want to draw their attention to me, in case they hadn't seen me yet.

But they had.

"Stop, or I'll shoot," hollered the one in front, who was about a metre away from me. I stopped right away. Without saying a word, I turned around, facing them, and handed over my cell phone and purse, even before they commanded me to do so. The one in the back stuffed my belongings onto his lap.

"Give us the money in your pockets," the same man grunted, "then leave right now." I pulled out five dollars, which he snatched from me. As they zoomed away, I thought: *Thank God. The only traumatic thing they did to me was point a gun in my face.*

I ran back to my mom's house and told her what had happened. She took me to the police station, where we learned that these guys were under investigation for crimes in her neighbourhood, but until then, the police had not had enough information to catch them.

While I was at the police station waiting to be heard, I kept thinking of what could have happened to me if I had reacted just a little bit differently. I wondered why God allowed something like that to happen, when all I was doing was trying to be better, to walk right. Instead of being with most of the people I knew, partying and getting drunk that day, I was going to a church event. Truth is, I still don't have the answer for why He allowed that to happen. But one thing I know, for sure: He spared me from being sexually assaulted or killed that afternoon. For that, I am eternally grateful.

Once we were done with the police, I asked my mother to take me to the retreat so I could finished what I started. When I got there, I was late. One of the guest speakers was at the door, checking the accreditations of those entering.

"Why did you miss almost half the workshop?" she asked me. I told her about the robbery. Later that night, as we talked a little more, we became friends. I told her the bank I worked for had its headquarters based in Fortaleza, the city where she lived, and that soon, I would be travelling there for a thirty-day course. I said I would love to know more about her religious community and to visit their evangelical centre. She gave me her home address and telephone number, and asked me to contact her once I arrived there, so that we could meet.

Chapter 5

Avoiding Discomfort: Another Feeble Excuse for Fear

"And when the servant of the man of God arose early and went out, there was an army, surrounding the city with horses and chariots. And his servant said to him, 'Alas, my master! What shall we do?' So he answered, 'Do not fear, for those who are with us are more than those who are with them.'"

2 Kings 6:15-16 (NKJV)

ONE DAY BEFORE MY TRIP to Fortaleza, I went to see Vania and gave her a hug. Since we had reconnected, this would be the first time we would stay far from each other for an extended period of time. As we said our goodbyes and she was hugging me, she told me something very interesting.

"You know, I had a vision," she said. "I saw you talking with a woman whose skin was very pale. You will meet her during this trip. Pay attention to her and what she has to tell you because she will teach you something really valuable."

I thought she was talking about my roommate for the soon-to-be course, a girl I will call Amanda. Although we had not yet met, we used to work in a different branch of the same bank, my former employer, in a state and city not far from my hometown. Days before the trip, I had found her name in the participants' list and contacted her, by email, asking if she would be interested in sharing a room in a hotel during the course, to minimize costs.

We both arrived in Fortaleza late at night. We had to be up early the next morning to be ready for our first class. Once we had gotten into our room, we faced our first disappointment: we had only one bed for the two of us. But we were so tired, we didn't mind sharing it for one night; we thought we could get it fixed later. When we turned on the air conditioning, we found out that it was broken. Since the room was extremely hot, we had no option but to open the window. But as we opened it, we were shocked by the outdoor noise; a few blocks away was a large concentration of prostitutes and sex-oriented businesses.

Since Amanda and I were exhausted, we just wanted to sleep and run away from that place in the morning. We thought things couldn't get worse, yet we found a huge cockroach between our bed sheets. There was nothing we could do. We wept in despair until sleep overtook us.

In the morning, as soon as the sun rose, we woke up and checked out. We had no idea where to go, but were determined not to spend another night in that horrible place. Since we didn't know the city and barely knew each other, we followed the others to a shuttle bus stop where the bank transported employees to and from the head office in ultra-comfortable buses. We hopped on the shuttle bus and went to our class, carrying our luggage with us.

When we got to the facility, I called a colleague who recommended a furnished apartment hotel a few blocks away from one of the company's bus stops. When we went there to check it out, we fell in love with it as soon as we got to the lobby; it was spacious and bright and furnished with fashionable items. The stay would obviously be more expensive but we made a deal with the manager; we told him that we had a class of twenty people coming from all parts of the country and if he gave us a discount, we would get them to move there. He agreed, giving us a deal for every room we would help him to rent. Before the end of the second day of the course, nine of us were sharing the last three apartments available. As Amanda and I didn't want to share with a third person, five guys got the second apartment and the remaining two women took the third and last one.

It felt like we were a big family, like we had known each other for a long time. Every day, we would walk to the bus station in the morning, have lunch together, and walk back to the hotel. Later, we would gather to study for the exams and laugh with everybody telling stories all night long. If one us wanted to go sightseeing or grocery shopping, the other eight people would come along, and we would always have something later to laugh about.

One Friday night, the other two women invited Amanda and me for a drink; it was a girls' night out. We talked about a lot of things but they turned the focus of conversation to me and my left hand.

"We noticed that you still had a mark from your wedding band on your finger," one of them said. "We're just curious. What happened?" I had never talked with or about Tom since my arrival.

I told them my story and shared my faith. To my surprise, they shared the same belief in Jesus and each had a sad story of her own. I noticed that one of the women, whom I will name Marisa, was so white we could easily see her veins in her face and arms. Vania's mention of her vision popped into my mind; she had said that I would have something to learn from this woman. I told Marisa about this.

"Do you believe that you're the person from Vania's vision?" I asked her.

"Yes." We didn't go farther than that.

Next day, Marisa knocked on our door. "There's something I didn't tell you about my life and I need to share it with you," she said. "I need your advice."

About ten years earlier, Marisa had broken up with her boyfriend. One of his ex-girlfriends was always calling and texting her, saying lies about she and him still seeing each other. Although Marisa knew that the woman was lying, she was afraid of getting into a fight and losing him, so she gave up. Months later, that woman got what she wanted; she was pregnant and they were getting married. Marisa then quit her job and moved to Rio.

"When I left him, I didn't know Jesus," she said. "During that dark time, when I was living alone in the capital, surrounded by bad influences, I hit bottom. But that's how I got saved."

After five years had passed, Marisa decided to return to her hometown. "I discovered that the love of my life was now divorced and fighting for custody of his daughter.

"We started dating again and soon after that, we got engaged. But a horrible tragedy happened. I can't tell you about it right now." She began to sniffle a little. "Can you believe that he passed away before the wedding day? The pain was excruciating, but the only way I could bear it was through my faith."

As she finished telling her story, we were all in tears. Although I was truly sad, I admit that hearing her made me realize how blessed I was. My problems seemed so insignificant compared to her suffering.

Amanda asked her: "What kind of advice were you looking for when you knocked at our door?"

Marisa told us that a few months before her trip to Fortaleza, a lawyer had visited her and given her the key to an apartment that her fiancé had bought, years ago, when they first dated, just before she broke up with him.

"He said that my fiancé had planned to surprise me with the keys on our wedding day."

The apartment was fully furnished and had pictures of her everywhere. "When I saw dead flowers in a vase, the housekeeper told me that once a week, my fiancé would go and change the flowers, even during the five years I was away, because he always knew that one day, we would be together again."

But now that he was gone, his ex-wife was getting ready to take Marisa to court and fight for the apartment. Even though the lawyer had said that she should not worry, because the woman had no legal rights, Marisa was still wondering if she should keep it or just give it away.

"I'm tired of fighting and losing," she said.

When I heard that, I felt the Holy Spirit say inside my heart, "Take possession of what is yours." Because her fiancé had put his love all over that apartment, giving up on it would be the same as rejecting his love. Fear had blinded her; she couldn't see that she had already won that battle and there was nothing that the other woman could do about it.

Although I thought I should learn something from Marisa, I realized that I was the one who could teach her something. I had been fighting all my life to survive and there I was, still fighting. So I told her what I felt the Holy Spirit said to me about her situation and what I believed she should do.

We all had a great time in Fortaleza and after we returned to our homes, we still kept exchanging emails for several months. But with time and because of our busy routines and the distance, we lost contact. I never heard from Marisa again. I had no idea then that her words would return to me later with striking significance.

That whole experience in Fortaleza certainly helped me a lot, in many ways, except for my work situation. Since I was promised a promotion, I agreed to work overtime, on a voluntary basis, to learn what I needed for the new position. Although they had told me that I would be ready to start as a sub-manager after that course in Fortaleza, five months had passed and I was still waiting.

So, one day, I took the plunge and asked the general manager what was going on.

"I'm very sorry," he said, "but the person you were going to replace changed his mind about resigning. We made a mistake announcing an opening for a position that was never available."

He never apologized for not letting me know as soon as he found out that they no longer had an opening. Nor for the eight months that I worked overtime for free, under the false impression that it was for a better future.

"You're irresponsible and immature," I roared at him, "and what you did was nasty. That's no way to treat a loyal, hard-working employee like me. It's unbelievable."

I had never yelled so much at anyone—not even my mother.

He threatened to call the superintendent to report my behaviour and get me suspended if I didn't apologize and stop yelling. Well, he didn't know me at all. I was trained to be cold and not to fear any kind of threat. He thought I would fall for that, but I did not.

"Go ahead and make the call," I replied, "and don't forget to add that I said I would never again work under your authority."

As always, I let anger dictate how I should react. I acted out of impulse. It didn't take me long to realize that it wasn't the right thing to do. Then I started to feel guilty and unworthy of God's love.

That day, as soon as I arrived home from work, I ran to Vania and told her how horrible I felt for not controlling my reactions.

I told her I was going backwards, becoming the person I used to be, and thought that was unacceptable for a Christian. With a smile on her face, Vania got up from her old rocking chair, grabbed her battered and scribbled-upon Bible, and opened it at the chapter where Jesus got upset over the people transforming the church into a marketplace:

So they came to Jerusalem. Then Jesus went into the temple and began to drive out those who bought and sold in the temple, and overturned the tables of the money changers and the seats of those who sold doves. And He would not allow anyone to carry wares through the temple. Then He taught, saying to them, "Is it not written, 'My house shall be called a house of prayer for all nations'? But you have made it a 'den of thieves.' (Mark 11:15-17 NKJV).

She didn't say that what I did was good, but showed me that as humans, we are sometimes caught in our emotions; since even Jesus had expressed anger, I should forgive myself and sin no more. That verse brought peace to my heart and made me see that there was so much more to learn about Jesus and his life, death, and resurrection.

I also learned that He is an awesome lawyer. The manager did take my case to the superintendent but I didn't know that he was famous for doing things like that. I was deemed in the right to stand up and confront him. So, instead of a suspension, which would have been registered in my employee file, I was told to take some vacation time to cool off, because how I had behaved wasn't appropriate.

A week later, the superintendent offered me a temporary transfer to another branch in a city much closer to Aracaju, where I would be substituting for a sub-manager who was going on vacation for a month.

"You need more time far away from that manager you blew up at," he told me. "And I wanted to find some way to repay you for all the extra hours you worked without pay. Have fun."

After I made sure that he had hung up, I started to scream so that the whole word, except him, could hear.

"God is faithful!" I cried. "God is faithful!

Chapter 6

Paid In Full: I Became Debt-free

"Now may He who supplies seed to the sower, and bread for food, supply and multiply the seed you have sown and increase the fruits of your righteousness."

2 Corinthians 9:10 (NKJV)

THINGS STARTED TO GET BETTER at work but not with my financial situation. After we separated, Tom stopped paying for the loan we had both gotten to build the house, which was being paid off every month from my bank account. In addition, I had rented a place I mistakenly thought I could pay for because of the promised promotion. My salary was not enough to pay for all that and for the luxuries I was used to buying. When my landlord said she didn't want to renew our agreement because I was usually late in my payments, I was caught off guard. I had less than two months to move out and didn't have any money or credit to rent anywhere else. So, I began to pray and asked God for his help.

One day, as I was praying, I remembered how good it was to share the apartment with Amanda in Fortaleza; I thought about all the things we went through on that horrible first night at the hotel. I realized that if Amanda and I had stayed at that hotel, we would never have done grocery shopping, cooking, cleaning or laundry together. Without that experience, I would never have come to the conclusion that the solution for my problem was to find someone to live with me and share expenses like she did. That was the only way I could afford a place and get out of debt.

All the people I knew were either married or living well with their parents. I had no other contacts. My best shot was the classifieds. Searching for a place close to Vania's apartment building, I found four college students looking for someone to replace one of the women who was about to graduate and travel back home.

I didn't like their apartment, but I did like them. They were nice women and really fun people to hang out with. All of them worked part-time and studied at night. They were about my age and loved to have people over for small gatherings. We chatted for almost two hours. However, I explained that I was looking for a much quieter environment and they understood. Just before I left, one of the women asked for my telephone number so that we could keep in touch.

My moving date was getting closer and I still hadn't found a new place. Perhaps my requirements were a little too hard to fulfill: I didn't want to live with more than one person, I wanted to be within walking distance from Vania, and my roommate had to be Christian. So, I started to get worried. Vania suggested that I list my requirements on a piece of paper and pray about them, asking God to send me that specific someone and to help us find a place where we could both help each other, not only financially but also so that we could grow in our faith.

One night, Kayla, my friend from high school, invited me to her father's birthday party. Because I no longer had a car, I needed her to come and pick me up. When she got to my place, she saw my things packed up.

"Have you found what you're looking for? She asked me, surveying my piles of boxes stacked high.

"No, but I quit worrying about that because I believe that God is doing all the searching for me."

She looked right at me. "Look, Sabrina, I admire your faith but you are very close to not having a place to live. Do you want to end up homeless? Maybe you should consider lowering your expectations regarding the person, place or both."

Less than a minute after she finished talking, my phone rang. A woman that I will call Lynn asked me if I was still looking for a place and person to move in with. She had visited the same apartment I had gone to, where those college students lived. When she said to them that she was looking to share a place with one person only, because she wanted a quieter environment, they thought about me right away. And that was how she got my phone number.

Kayla and I were amazed. Yes, we believed in miracles, but that was too crazy good to believe.

But after some unexplainable joy, a huge fear gripped my heart. Who was this woman? How could I trust that she was good? Why was she looking for a place? What was her story? So many questions started to bother me, and something that had made me so happy, only a few minutes later, was now making me feel very sad.

I had to keep reminding myself that I had left that matter in God's hands. If He was taking care of it, I should trust that He knew best, even when I didn't know a thing. So, I agreed to meet her in a week. I also asked for her email address so that we could keep in touch until then.

After the party for Kayla's dad, I went home and couldn't stop thinking how amazing this synchronicity was. Before I went to bed, I prayed for a sign that Lynn was the person I'd been asking Him to find for me. During my prayer, I felt such peace that I ended up falling asleep.

In the morning, as soon as I got to work, I wrote Lynn an email, asking her to tell me a little bit about herself and her motives for wanting to move in with a complete stranger. Then, the sign I had prayed about the night before, came in her reply.

Lynn was an entrepreneur; she was opening a student travel and education agency in my city. She already owned an agency in her town and wanted to expand the business, reaching Aracaju first because of its potential market. Well, that was good. I found out she worked and consequently, could afford her part of the bills. But I still didn't know if she was a good person, if she was "my person." So, she wrote another email, saying: "I spent last night praying for a sign because I didn't know if I was doing the right thing. Please understand that I am still not sure yet about us sharing a place."

What? To me, that was totally a sign. I told her, "Since we spoke on the phone, I was also praying and asking for the same thing: a sign that you were the right person to share a place with me. The reason why I haven't found a roommate is because one of my requirements is to find someone who believes in God as much as I do, if not more."

Fifteen days later, we found an amazing apartment in the best location and for a very good deal. Check mark! God had fulfilled every single requirement on my list.

With time, I learned that Lynn and her fiancé were leaders of a youth group at her church. For the entire year that we shared the apartment, we talked about God and his goodness. She taught me a lot about the stories in the Bible and tales of lives that were changed in her ministry. I was blessed. She also talked to me about her business and about other cultures. She showed me a lot of pictures of the places around the world where she had been.

Without noticing it, she had stirred up in my heart a dream that I have had since I was little. I used to love reading books. Fiction, poems, and world history books were my favourites. Every time that I read about some country's history, I would say: "One day, I will see the entire world, no longer from these pictures, but with my own eyes."

I wanted to speak other languages and eat different foods. I wanted to meet all kinds of people and learn from them. I always knew that I was not meant to be where I was, but could never see a way out. Either my mother would drag me down, saying it was impossible for people like us to do such a thing or Tom and his family would laugh at me, saying: "You're a dreamer and should accept your reality."

Lynn showed me the way. As she presented to me the number of people who travel every year to a different country, she proved my mom wrong. "Many have done it already," she said. She also told me that more and more, lack of international experience was becoming a deal breaker when big companies were considering hiring someone. They would most likely hire a person with a global perspective who speaks another language because it was easier to achieve broader goals if someone could view things through the lens of another culture. Cultural exchange programs were the new trend, more a reality than a dream.

Lynn knew all about my past and financial situation. She suggested: "Why don't you sell your part in the house to Tom and use the money to pay off your debts and take a trip to Europe?" I liked the idea, but selling the house was not an option because my divorce papers were not signed yet and I didn't have the money to hire a lawyer. But I was determined to save as much money as I could. Even if took me ten years, I would go on that trip.

I started to put my plan into action. At work, after my thirty days of substitution ended, another sub-manager went on vacation. Because I was already there and knew the procedure, they allowed me to stay for another month, working in his place. That extra money helped me to bring a lot of small debts up to date. But more than half of my pay was going to the loan and rent, and I still had to buy food and pay for transportation. It seemed like it would take a lot more than ten years to be completely debt free and have enough to afford my adventure.

As crazy as it sounds, that was when I began to tithe my earnings to the church. Reading that same book I bought, which had led me to Jesus, I read a chapter about trusting God with my finances. The author mentioned a verse in the Bible where God asked us to test Him. I first thought that something was wrong. I didn't know all the Bible verses, but I did know the one where Jesus said to Satan, when he was being tempted, that we should not test the Lord our God: *"And Jesus answered and said to him, 'It has been said, 'You shall not tempt the Lord your God' "* (Luke 4:12 (NKJV)).

So, I took my Bible and looked for that first verse.

To my surprise, I found out that God, indeed, said to bring the tithe to his house and He would bless us in a way whereby we wouldn't have room enough to store it. I read: *Bring all the tithes into the storehouse, that there may be food in My house, and try Me now in this, says the Lord of hosts, "If I will not open for you the windows of heaven. And pour out for you such blessing that there will not be room enough to receive it."* (Malachi 3:10 (NKJV))

That same month, I managed to do a smaller grocery shopping and for the first time in my life, I gave ten per cent of my income to my local church.

Sure enough, my financial situation started to turn around. The sub-manager I was substituting for never came back from vacation and the person designated to take his place was not able to take over his new role for almost six months. That left me there, filling up the gap. It took so long for him to show up that I even thought God wanted me to be the sub-manager for good. But close to the end of the sixth month, the new guy arrived. The thought that I would have to return to the old branch and the old manager started to hurt me in my Soul.

I didn't want to see that man again or leave behind the new friends that I had made. I asked Jesus to help me to forgive and let go of the past because I had no other option. I needed to work and that was the place I was assigned, regardless of my feelings. As much as I hated the idea, I was aware that I had to apologize. I knew what God expected me to do and I was trying to be obedient.

So, I called that man and said, "I shouldn't have raised my voice to you. For that, I want to say, 'sorry'."

I bet he didn't see that coming. After some awkward silence, he said, "I'm also very sorry for the way I handled the situation. If you want to come back, I will make up for it somehow."

But I didn't want to go back. I didn't want to go back at all.

Calling him and apologizing was a huge step for a new Christian, but asking me to believe that he would keep his word and make up for what he had done to me was a little too much. So I begged to stay where I was. They agreed but the only position available at that branch was as a teller. That meant I would be going down, one level, from my original position before the fight, but I was so desperate that I accepted.

Since I was about to lose access to running credit reports and credit scores, I decided to take a look into mine and see how much my situation had improved since I started paying back a lot of my old debts. But, instead of improvement, I saw a lot of new debts that I didn't make. After some investigation, I found out that those two men on a motorcycle, who took my purse at gunpoint years ago, used my documents as fake ID to get approved for credit cards. Four of the major banks in Brazil gave them credit without verifying my signature. Because the authorities didn't have the right address or telephone number for me, I was never contacted. If it weren't for me running those reports, I would never have known anything about it.

In my new position as a teller, I had to talk to customers every day. I was right at the door, the first person they would see as they entered the bank. (Before, as an analyst, I never had to talk to a customer because I used to work internally approving, or not, mortgages and loans. As a sub-manager, I was responsible for going after those who were not paying their debts; because they were the minority and hid from us most of the time, I would rarely talk to them either.)

But work as a teller helped me to get to know a lot of new people: most importantly, a man I will call James. I saw him many times, accompanying his clients to cash their compensation for punitive damages. He was a famous lawyer, known for never losing a case against financial institutions. He was really good, and was aware of it. When he agreed to take my case, I was nervous about the attorney's fees but he promised that I didn't need to pay him a penny if he lost my case. I would only pay him if he won. Then, I would give him a percentage of my gains.

James was also a sweetheart. We became very close friends. He helped me get my divorce finalized and, again, didn't charge for it until I received my first compensation. It took us about a year and a half but we received everything the judge determined.

With the money I got, I was able to pay off the loan and all of my remaining debts. Finally, I was debt free! Not only that, but with that money, I was also able to help people around me who were in need of a financial breakthrough, like I had been.

It would have taken me ten years if it weren't for God turning around a harmful situation into a blessing. It was one that I could never have imagined, even in my best dreams.

Chapter 7

Best Friends for Life

"Let all bitterness, wrath, anger, clamour, and evil speaking be put away from you, with all malice. And be kind to one another, tenderhearted, forgiving one another, even as God in Christ forgave you."

Ephesians 4:31-32 (NKJV)

ONCE I HAD PAID OFF everything I owed, my attitude about how I was spending money changed a lot. In the past, not being able to use a credit card and only paying for things I could afford, in cash, taught me a lot. The desire to go on a trip for a year around Europe also became more reachable and I needed to save money for that. Since I didn't have much left over from my salary, I decided to cut down my expenses even more than before.

To do that, I had to move one more time. I needed an apartment with cheaper rent; since Lynn didn't want to move with me, I had to look for another roommate. I already knew the drill regarding what I had to do to find the right person. I prayed and waited patiently, trusting that the same God who helped me before would help me again.

One day, when I was chatting online with a friend from church, she asked me if I was still living at the same address. I told her yes, but that I wanted to move to a place with cheaper rent, in a nice and safe neighbourhood, and that I would need a new roommate. To my delight, she told me about her colleague from college, a Christian and very friendly woman who was looking for another woman to share the rent. The location of her apartment was great, just across the street from the church and one block away from Vania. I didn't think twice. Immediately, I grabbed all the information I needed, jumped from my chair, and called the woman, whom I will call Dora.

We talked a little bit over the phone and after that, met at her place on that same day. The apartment was nice and tidy and she was truly very friendly, but she needed someone to move in as soon as possible. I still had two months left on my lease.

Those two months passed very fast. I had only one week left in the apartment with Lynn. I had no idea what to do next. I was already contemplating the idea of living with my mom's parents for a while when my phone rang.

It was Dora. The roommate she had had for the past two months caused her nothing but trouble, so she had to let her go. She wondered if I was still looking for a place and if I could consider her offer to move to her apartment and share expenses with her.

I was grateful that she called. I moved to her apartment a week after that. A couple of months later, we were sharing our stories, crying together, laughing about silly things, polishing our nails, and learning more about God. We became very good friends.

During the time we shared the apartment, I was able to save money and had the opportunity to travel to a lot of places within Brazil. I was always looking for a chance where I could be in a different place and meet new people, as I was preparing my spirit for a bigger and longer trip.

My life was getting better and better but I still had a lot of unresolved issues in my head. Much of it had to do with my mother and the anger I harboured against her. So, I kept praying for help. One day, at work, we all received an email with an advertisement for a weekly free theatre class, on Saturday mornings, hosted by the federal university. Because I had always loved to be part of plays during my childhood, I decided to sign up for these classes. I needed a hobby and that was an opportunity to get to know a lot of different people.

When I arrived for my first class, I was welcomed by the one of the teachers, who I will call Gordon. He apologized that his fiancé, who I will call Karie, also a teacher, couldn't be present because she had been the victim of a car accident. He explained that they were both psychologists. Their plan for our group was to help us explore our own problems due to abuse and perhaps help us solve them by using theatre techniques.

While he was talking about the accident, I couldn't help but notice Gordon's Christian-based speech. That surprised me a lot because I had looked for a psychologist for a while and had to give up; every time I would tell them that Jesus and I used to talk, they would look at me in a concerned way, and say that I was at the wrong place, that I needed a psychiatrist instead.

I felt in my heart that I should talk to Gordon after class. I waited for everyone to leave and approached him, using the same question that I had asked other psychologists before, to identify if he was the right person to help me.

"Do you believe that God can talk to me?"

"I do, because He talks to me too."

I was covered in goose bumps.

After that answer, I knew that Gordon was the person I was looking for. He agreed to start treating me as soon as possible. The sessions were mostly outdoors; I had a favourite place, a park by the river where I used to go to jog or ride a bicycle. He would meet me there, once a week, and we would walk and talk for an hour. We only met at his office, when it happened to be raining, which was almost never.

In the meantime, the theatre group was getting bigger. New people were coming every weekend. That was awesome; we all had some sort of issues to deal with. Because of that, newcomers and veterans had no difficult bonding. During the sessions, we would recreate a scene or story in which each us had been abused. Group participants would come up with a different ending for our stories by suggesting different reactions we could have had when the abuse happened. By doing this, I learned that many times, I could have avoided some of these situations if I had said "no" more times, had learned to ignore people and their words, or simply left. Not surprisingly, because of what I was learning, positive results started to appear, very quickly, in my life.

Every time I had a therapy session, we would start with a prayer. I was always asking God to use Gordon's skills and wisdom as a tool to show me what I couldn't see on my own. With Gordon's help, I could address issues such as why, despite all of my efforts, I never learned how to love Tom. Or why was I never satisfied with anything I did or achieved? The reason was clear, I just couldn't see it until then: I was always doing things to please people, not to please God.

"But how could I please Him if I did not even know Him then?" I once asked Gordon.

"Well, you know Him now, don't you?" he answered.

That changed my thinking and way of doing things. Mostly, it changed my conversation with my Heavenly Father. I was always asking for help after I had already done things, but I never asked for His advice before I jumped into something. So, I decided to let go of my container of old views and ways and allow God to pour out His blessings into a fresh and new container. I needed a new heart.

The first thing I needed to do was to forgive my mother. I would never truly be able to become what I was meant to be, while I maintained the attitude that I should prove her wrong and show her how successful I turned out to be. It wasn't easy. I started to visit her more often and had to hear a lot of offensive comments and insults. Quietly, many times, I thought about giving up. But then,

I was reminded that I was not doing this for her or for me—I was doing it for God. He had promised to help me through the trials.

I kept praying and visiting my mother. Sometimes, I would fall into temptation and get into a fight with her. But I would soon realize that it was a trap and would humble myself, asking for forgiveness, even when I knew I was right. She kept hurting me with her harsh words and lack of respect until one day, something crazy happened to me.

One night, Vania and I were together with other members of our charismatic group, praying for one another. I told them I was not feeling well. I suddenly became very weak. Vania quickly asked them to gather in a circle around me and to pray for my recovery. All of a sudden, I started to feel my body getting heavier. I completely lost control of it, falling on my back onto a concrete floor. Apparently, according to those present, the noise of my body falling was so loud that it scared passersby.

I don't remember hearing anything, but I got up from the floor very scared. I ran to Vania, who hugged me and asked me to be calm. When I could finally speak, my first words were "*I want my mom.*".

As crazy as it sounds, I didn't feel any pain, not at the time of the fall or ever. Vania told me it was the Holy Spirit in action. God was healing me from all the pain I went through because of all the wrong things my mother did or said to me. He was setting me free from all of my resentment. The Bible says: *"Then they laid hands on them, and they received the Holy Spirit"* (Acts 8:17 (NKJV)).

I spent twenty-seven years thinking that my mother didn't love me or want me around. I fought as hard as I could to change her. At first, I would yell at her, to show her that she hurt me, expecting that she would apologize and never do that again. Well, it didn't work. So, I started to answer her back with attitude and that made her even angrier. I soon realized that didn't work either. So, I decided to shut her out of my life, trying to do things the way I thought was right. It didn't matter if she said the opposite; my intention was always to prove her wrong.

When I met Jesus, I started to pray and ask him to change her heart. It was my last resort, but even that didn't work. Not because Jesus couldn't do it, but because it wasn't his plan at the moment. He wanted to change me, instead. Sure enough, after the day I fell to the ground, my relationship with my mom started to get better. It was not because she changed and became a perfect mother—she is still the same even today— but because I forgave her.

Not having those feelings towards her helped me to understand where she came from and how she learned to love and care. I began to know her more deeply so, after that, when she used a harsh word or offend me, I would focus on what she meant to say, instead of what she actually said. I finally realized what God meant when He said that if we want a better and longer life, we should honour our parents. As a result of respecting my mother's authority, I began to earn her respect. We started to trust each other and learned to deal with our differences a lot better than before. We became the best friends in the world.

One year after that, on my birthday, my mom wrote me an email, saying that the happiest day of her life was when I was born. For the first time in many years, she said she loved me. Wow! God is truly an amazing Healer. He first worked on my heart; by changing me, He changed my circumstances.

I love my mother, and thank God, every day, for her life.

This book could end here. I could say that was the biggest lesson of my life and that having my mother's friendship was the greatest gift God could ever give to me, but his goodness is immeasurable and He always keeps his promises. On the night I woke up with Him calling me, He made me a promise to take care of each one of my worries. He took care of my debts, then restored my relationship with my mother. But I still didn't know what to do with my professional and personal life; I didn't know which career path to follow. I had half of a house that I couldn't sell or live in. And I really wanted to have my own family.

As it is written in the Bible, He had planned something bigger and better than I could have ever imagined or asked for.

"Now to Him who is able to do exceedingly abundantly above all that we ask or think, according to the power that works in us, to Him be glory in the church by Christ Jesus to all generations, forever and ever. Amen" (Ephesians 3:20-21 (NKJV)).

Chapter 8

The Real Planner

"There are many plans in a man's heart, Nevertheless the Lord's counsel—that will stand."

Proverbs 19:21 (NKJV)

MY WORK AT THE BANK was never something I always wanted or liked doing. I had only applied for that job because I wanted to be free from Tom and my mother's oppressive influence. After I got officially divorced and my mother and I became friends, there was nothing to keep me from quitting that job. I had all my debts paid, I was spending less money than I was making, and was able to start a savings account.

It was time to become who I was really meant to be. I felt the Holy Spirit guiding me to go back to university, but I didn't know which career I should pursue. I knew I wanted to travel around the world and definitely wouldn't grow older living in Aracaju. Both Vania and Gordon had told me, many times, that I should write a book; I had always loved to read and write. At church, the elders in the group invited me to preach the Gospel and people were responding positively. I brought that all into consideration and thought that I should go for a psychology degree. But it didn't feel quite right. I didn't have peace in my heart; every time I thought about it, I would feel nauseous, like something awful was about to take place. I began to pray about it, and asked God to reveal his will, to show me not only which career to start but also how I should start. I didn't want to pay for another course or get any kind of loan.

As a result of my prayer, I heard God's voice, deep inside of my heart, asking me to think about the things I loved to do when I was a teenager.

The answer came quickly.

I used to spend hours translating songs from English to Portuguese. One of my biggest passions was to learn and teach English. Then, I felt the Holy Spirit prompting me to apply for a tuition-free public university. I thought that was impossible; only with a miracle could I get in. First, because of the high competitiveness and number of candidates per vacancy, and second, because of the entrance exam. I would be vying for a vacancy against student opponents who were just finishing high school and I had already graduated ten years beforehand. It was a lot easier for them to remember what they had learned than for me. But I did it anyway. At the last minute, I submitted my application for an English language and literature degree.

Here's how the entrance exam process ("Vestibular"), which we go through to get into several universities in Brazil, works; it's divided into two phases. The first phase consists of three days of exams. Each day, we have to answer different questions about the same ten subjects that we have all studied at high school, such as math, history and literature. Day after day, the level of difficulty for these questions gradually increases.

Every subject has a different weight of scoring, according to which graduation course we are applying for. So, a zero in biology would affect someone applying for medicine, but not me, for example. Even so, to get to the second phase, candidates have to make sure that during the previous three days of exams, they did not get a zero on more than two tests in any of the subjects.

The second phase consists of an essay we have to write, based on a theme provided at the time we open our envelopes. After that, a group of university teachers will read it and give it a score. At the end of the process, all the scores are added up. The candidates with the highest scores are the ones who will fill the vacancies, in descending order, up to the maximum number available.

I was always very good in math. Even if I wasn't that great, I had to be at least good to work for a bank. But somehow, I managed to get zero on two tests during the first two days of math exams. My siblings were both going through the same process to get into the same public university. My little brother was pursuing an engineering degree and my sister, business administration. Both needed a high score in mathematics so I asked them to give me some hints. They spent the night before our last exam studying with me and made me feel confident, but it didn't prevent me from getting another zero.

It was over. I was eliminated and also very embarrassed.

There was nothing I could do about it. I decided to go and watch a movie; it was a famous Christian film about God doing the impossible in the lives of a couple who were struggling with work, finances, and starting a family. I was halfway through the movie when my little brother called me to say that some students were questioning the results for the last math exam. If they were right, the university would have to give away some points to each candidate and that could bring me back into the game. I was speechless. I knew I needed a miracle to pass the exams but that was incredible.

So, I passed. I was ranked twenty-sixth among all candidates who got each of the fifty vacancies available for the English language and literature course. If that wasn't already something amazing enough to give glory to God for, imagine how I felt when I found out that my siblings had passed as well.

For the first time, in our town, three siblings got accepted to the same public university, in the same year. If that wasn't a miracle, what could be? In one day I was eliminated, and on the following day, He not only brought me back into the game, but gave me victory. And He put me and my family into a place of honour before the entire city.

Classes started on February 2009 and I was doing great. After some months speaking and learning English, I thought I had it all figured out: I would save money until December, then quit my work and go on a trip to Europe. I'd stay a little while in London, where I could practice the language more, and after a year, I would be back to finish university and start teaching. As a teacher, I could impact the life of my students and bring them closer to Jesus. That was how I would serve him.

Well, that was my plan. But God's plans for me were a lot different.

Sergipe is the smallest state in Brazil; we are a much laid-back population, mostly formed by farmers. Very rarely do we host a big event or concerts; for that, we usually travel to Bahia, a state very close that is also very popular, even more so after the 2014 World Cup. But in Sergipe, more specifically in Aracaju City, the Brazilian Gymnastics Federation established its site. Because of that, in November 2009, Aracaju hosted the Junior Pan-American Championships in gymnastics for the first time.

Someone from my class emailed the entire group with information and deadlines for those who wanted to volunteer as interpreters at the event. I thought it would be a great opportunity to practice my English and gather some experience since I was planning to apply for a work opportunity, as a volunteer, at the 2014 Olympic Games in London.

So, I sent my application to the Federation. A few days later, I was invited for an interview. There were about forty people searching for an opportunity to be part of that event. They narrowed us down to twenty, and from that number, they shortlisted ten of us. From these ten people, six should be able to speak fluent Spanish and the other four, fluent English.

All of the candidates competing for the English vacancies, except me, had previously lived in the U.S., England or Canada for at least a year. I didn't know what frustrated me the most, the fact that they were all a lot younger than I and had already accumulated that kind of experience, or that I choked in my interview, intimidated by them.

I left the meeting so upset and frustrated. I knew it was just one of the many opportunities I could have in the future, but for some reason, I really wanted to be part of that event. And so did our Heavenly Father. And when He plans something for us, He moves mountains and makes impossible things possible. I thought of this Biblical verse:

So Jesus said to them, "Because of your unbelief; for assuredly, I say to you, if you have faith as a mustard seed, you will say to this mountain, 'Move from here to there,' and it will move; and nothing will be impossible for you'." (Matthew 17:20 (NKJV).

Even though I had a horrible interview, after two days, they called me. I was selected. The person coordinating the interviews was one of my classmates. I didn't recognize her because she took only one class with me, but she did remember me and according to her, she knew how well I was doing in the course. She figured that

I was just nervous at the interview, so she called me anyway.

When I sent in the application form, I let the Brazilian Federation know that I was available to help only on the weekend, because on week days I was usually very busy working and studying all day. So, they assigned me to look after the U.S. team just for the opening and closing ceremony.

The delegations arrived on Monday, November 2, a national holiday in Brazil. Since I was off work, I decided to go to the hotel and help the other volunteers with the athletes' and coaches' accreditation. And that was how I met the man I love, my husband, Frank. One of the Canadian coaches, he was so young, and all the other coaches around so much older, I thought Frank was an athlete. So, when he tried to start a conversation with me, kind of flirting, I laughed and ignored him, thinking that he should grow a little older for that.

That should have been the first, and perhaps last, time that we saw each other; I was hardly there, since I was responsible for Team USA for only a few hours on two nights. But the volunteer in charge of Team Canada didn't show up for his duty and the guy helping me with Team USA wasn't able to care for the two teams all day for the entire week. So, I was asked to help him out. He would be with both teams from morning until mid-afternoon, when I would finish my work at the bank and could be with them until the end of the shift, in the evening.

It was one of the busiest weeks of my life. I went to bed around 3:00 a.m. and would wake up two hours later to go to work. Then, from work, I would run to the gymnasium to cover the other volunteer. Even though it was a little hard for me, I was still very grateful because it was indeed an excellent opportunity to learn and to make friends. Everybody was amazed by the weather, our beaches, our people, and the parties. (I bet you have heard about our parties, but I can assure you that although it is true we Brazilians know how to host great events, it isn't always true that the women will be wearing only feathers and bikinis.) It was inevitable, for all of us, to have fun while we were working with so many people, from so many different nations. That led Frank and I to have a great time together. But at the beginning of our relationship, we ended up spending a lot more time together than I wanted.

Chapter 9

We Speak English in Canada

"Trust in the Lord with all your heart, And lean not on your own understanding; In all your ways acknowledge Him, And He shall direct your paths."

Proverbs 3:5-6 (NKJV)

SOME PEOPLE HAVE THE IMPRESSION that when we become Christians, we stop sinning instantly and forever. But I am here to let you know they are wrong. Even though I experienced the most amazing things that only God was able to do, I still had difficulty trusting my entire life to Him.

I was a control freak. Letting go was, without a doubt, the hardest thing for me to do. For example, I really wanted to have a family. I knew what the Bible said about being divorced; I also knew I had a promised that one day, God would give me a family. But I couldn't wait. Even though I knew I was acting wrong, that didn't keep me from looking for a person who would help me erase my past, forget my bad experiences, and give me the family I've always dreamed about.

Before meeting Frank, it took me almost four years of jumping from one relationship to another, trying to find the perfect guy, until I decided to stop and wait—not because I had learned the lesson, but because I wanted to avoid pain.

None of those relationships lasted longer than a month. Only one lasted for thirty-one days. I truly believed that I had finally found the right person. Yet, on the day after we completed our first "anniversary," the guy dumped me by text message. I was so heartbroken, yet knew it was my fault. If I wasn't desperate to find a perfect guy; I would have waited for someone who wanted something more serious. Therefore, I ended up hurting myself. I began to doubt God's ability to forgive my past mistakes. I thought I couldn't have a relationship because I had had one and blew it up.

So, when I met Frank, I had all these invisible walls built around me to prevent me from getting hurt again. He tried a couple of times to get to know me better and I avoided him, letting him know that I was there, spending time with him, because that was part of my work.

Then he took a different approach: he wanted to be just friends. (That is how Frank usually is; he never gives up easily on things and I thank God for that.) One day, during our commute from the gymnasium to the hotel, Frank sat beside me on the bus. He showed me a picture of his newborn niece.

"Isn't she a sweetie?" he asked me. "I've only got one sister and this is her first child."

She was the cutest thing ever: blonde and with beautiful blue eyes, like a mini-version of Frank. "She is adorable" I said. He also showed me pictures of his parents. "They were from Hungary and went through so much to get to Canada and start a better life there."

Frank explained how they wanted to give him and his sister a better quality of life and an opportunity for them to flourish in their career as gymnastics coaches. Frank, his sister, and his parents had practised gymnastics when they were younger and had represented Hungary in many international competitions. When they retired from their career as athletes, they became coaches, but there was only one gymnasium in the town where they had lived in Hungary, which made it almost impossible for them to work and make a good living from the sport they all loved. It warmed my heart to hear how close Frank was to his family and how much their work meant to them. It was such a good conversation that we didn't notice the hours advancing. We were already at the hotel when we realized it was about 3:00 a.m. Frank and I were sitting on chaise lounges, outside the building by the swimming pool area, when we heard weird splashing coming from inside the pool. Since we were alone and didn't see anybody coming out of the lobby, we got up from our chairs in a heartbeat. Was it an intruder? Who was using the pool at this hour?

As we raced back to the entrance, we saw a huge ball of fur getting out of the pool. We couldn't believe what we were seeing and neither could Mr. Rat, it appeared. Completely soaked, with water dripping from his whiskers, he stared at us with a look that seemed to say, "Shouldn't you two be in your rooms, sleeping, at this time of day?

In the following days, our long conversations, not the swimming rat, became a routine until early morning. As we sat by the pool, enjoying the breeze and the sound of the waves coming and going, it was all a perfect background for Frank's stories. How I loved to spend time hearing him talk. I still do. I would look deep inside his sky blue eyes and he would look back so open and sincerely. He was a lot different than any other man I'd been with. He didn't brag about his achievements or give me a sales job about all his qualities, trying to make me change my mind about us becoming a couple. Somehow, he felt safe and secure enough to share things that he did and wasn't proud of, how sorry he was for that, and how he wanted to change and become someone new. He was a good man. I could see that by how he honoured his parents and cared for his athlete. I had the opportunity to meet at least twenty other coaches but none of them had a relationship with their athletes like Frank had with his gymnast; it was like father and son.

But what really impressed me was the way he used to look at me. Every time he looked into my eyes, I felt something that I never experienced before. I felt admired. He was so respectful. Other guys, even my ex, would always look at me with desire and lust. I have to confess that at first, I used to like that; I wanted to be noticed. But then I realized that I was just another object, a trophy that they wanted to exhibit to show how good they were. Frank was not like that, perhaps because he had already collected so many trophies throughout his career.

He started to train in gymnastics when he was six years old. At age thirteen, he was already a member of the national team in Hungary. He won many national and international competitions and was very close to achieving his dream of competing at the Summer Olympics in

Sydney, Australia. But for that, he would have had to stay alone in Hungary, while his parents and sister moved to Canada. Frank chose to stay close to his parents and retired as an athlete. He began to coach boys in his new home country of Canada. It didn't take long for him to succeed in this new career: after coaching for only four years, Frank had his first national team athlete. Later, he became the only coach in British Columbia who won the title of best gymnastics coach of the year for seven consecutive years. Within the first fifteen years of his career, he garnered ten athletes in the national team.

By the end of that week, I was completely in love with him. I knew he shared the same feelings, and I wanted to tell him how special he was for me, but I couldn't. He was so handsome and amazing, it was hard to resist his charm. But he would be leaving Brazil in two days and I would be left, again, with a broken heart. So, I prayed and asked God to give me strength. I was determined to keep our relationship as it was, regardless of what we were feeling for each other.

It was the first time I let God be part of my relationship with a man. (Previously in prayer, I had asked God to guard my heart from being broken again, to show me if it was right to pursue a certain relationship, or if the wise thing to do was to keep a distance from it.) And once again, as in every other area of my life, He answered my prayer by giving me something different, something far better than I could expect.

On Saturday morning, a day before the farewell party, Frank and I decided to walk along the beach, to enjoy the beautiful sunshine and talk a bit more about ourselves, before the competition started. Halfway back to the hotel, he stopped me and asked, "Why don't you give me a chance? It seems to me like you've got feelings for me. Am I right?" "Well . . ." I looked down at the sand, then up at him. "You're right. I am in love with you. But that scares the heck out of me."

I told Frank my whole story, from the beginning, and why I thought it would be better for me to leave things the way they were, so that neither of us would get hurt. I thought that sharing my past with him would make him understand my reasons and agree to leave things as they were. He was surprised to learn that I was so young and had gone through so much already.

"Why are you so sure that we would hurt each other?" he asked me.

"Well, here's what I think is going to happen," I said, while holding his hand and looking into his eyes. "A few days after you get back to Canada, and back into your routine, I'll be nothing more than a good memory from one of your trips around the world."

Frank shook his head No and took my other hand in his. I continued. "As for me, I'll be the one bearing the pain of yet another short relationship that will end regardless."

But Frank was determined to win. His persistence amazed me; it seemed that no matter what I said, he had an answer ready. He would not take No for an answer. Trying to make me change my mind, he reminded me about my dream of travelling to London and practicing my English there. Then, with the cutest smile, he said: "You know what? In Canada we also speak English." He invited me to move to Vancouver, on Canada's west coast. That way, we would continue to see each other and get to know where our relationship could take us.

All I wanted to do in that moment was to jump into his arms and kiss him. But I didn't. I knew it would take me at least three years of saving money to have enough to afford a trip like that to Canada. By then, he would probably be married to someone else.

I was ready to explain my financial situation to him when my cell phone rang. It was James, my lawyer. One of the banks we had sued forgot to remove the debt made on my name from the credit report, even though they had paid me a fair amount of money in the past. Because they didn't fulfill their part of our agreement, the judge imposed a fine that was three times higher than the previous amount they had to pay me. James was calling to tell me the money would be available, in cash, in a couple of months.

And there, with the phone still in my hands and James still talking, I felt God's presence. I knew deep in my heart that this was the answer to my prayer. He wanted me to use that money to go to Canada.

Frank didn't know what was going on or why I was crying. As soon as I finished talking to James, I told him about the robbery, the lawyer, the debts, and the amount of money I was about to receive. After telling him my story, I asked him: "Are you sure you want me to go to Canada?"

He was so happy to hear that we could be together. I was even more so. I knew that even though he would be gone after the competition was over, it would not be the end, but the beginning of our story together. We kissed for the first time. It was the best feeling I have ever had. I didn't have to worry about him crossing the line sexually because I knew him so well and how much he respected me. I was certain that I could trust him and that made such a difference. I could enjoy the moment freely and to the fullest.

We spent the last two days enjoying ourselves and making plans for the future. But as the time of his departure got closer, it was as if I had forgotten all those plans, the good things we shared, and those signs that had led me to him. I allowed fear to settle in my heart and many doubting thoughts began to steal my peace and joy.

As I watched Frank through the airport's glass windows, waving goodbye as he walked towards the airplane, it really opened up a huge can of worms inside my brain. I started to think that we would never be able to see or hear from each other again, that our busy routines would keep us apart. Or perhaps I would have my visa denied and would not be able to visit him in Canada.

Immersed in my doubt and fear, I lost sight of Frank as he entered the plane. Because I didn't have enough strength to watch the plane take off, I turned around and started to walk towards what I thought would be my reality.

And then, I was saved by my phone again.

As I felt it vibrating, I took it out of my purse. There, I found a text message, the first of millions. It was from Frank, saying: "I miss you already" and "I love you." I could feel my heart almost jumping out of my mouth. I cried like a baby, but this time, I was no longer sad or doubting that we would be together again. These were tears of happiness.

After that message, I realized that I can't avoid fear, but it will grow only as much as I nourish it.

I decided to no longer let fear control my mind. I left the airport and went straight to the DPF (Brazilian Federal Police Department) to get my first passport issued. After all, I would need one to enter Canada, my new destination.

Frank's flight had three stops before he finally arrived in Vancouver. He kept texting me from each stop. After that, we talked on the phone every day, at all times through the day, by email. In the evening, Vancouver time, after he finished work, we would chat online, through the web camera, for about an hour. Since Brazil is five hours ahead of Vancouver, he would be calling me at 1:30 a.m. That was early, but I can assure you there was no better way to be woken up, in the middle of my sleep, than hearing Frank's voice.

Chapter 10

Antagonists: Every Good Story Has Them

"What then shall we say to these things? If God is for us, who can be against us?"

Romans 8:31 (NKJV)

AFTER A COUPLE OF DAYS, my passport was ready. It was time to take my decision to the next level. Until then, the trip to Canada was just a possibility, a dream, and we all know it is a lot easier to dream than to face the events of real life. Once I applied for a visa, I would have to deal with the consequences of my choice; my entire life would change radically. (I applied for a visitor visa, which would allow me to stay for six months with possible renewal for another six months.) If Canadian Immigration decided to accept my request, I would have to leave everything behind. That meant starting a new life in Canada—or in Brazil, if I had to go back. If they declined my request, I would have to leave in the past Frank and all that we had felt and shared together. And that was something that I didn't want to do. It was a very difficult decision to make; it seemed that I would lose either way. I realized that I couldn't decide, not alone anyway.

So, I looked to the Lord for help and the answers started to come in the most amazing ways. One time, a girl at church told me she had a vision of me, as a happy child, playing at a park, swinging high and freely because I knew my Father (God) was there to catch me if I needed. One night, I woke up with a text message on my phone, saying something like "Don't postpone your dreams. Tomorrow can be too late." Curiously, it came from someone I barely knew. As I texted back, asking who it was, the person replied, saying his name. The only person I knew with that name was one of my sister's high school friends. But until that moment, nobody in my family knew about my plans to leave Brazil. I hadn't told my friends either, let alone hers.

Even today, I still wonder how he got my telephone number.

Just like that, a lot of coincidences (I call them providences) led me to fully understand that it was God's will for me to go to Canada. I should have known that from the beginning, when I first prayed, asking for help and being told about the unexpected money that could pay for travel.

Because of the emotional scars I had accumulated throughout life, after the many times I was wrong and entered a relationship or jumped into something that I would later regret, I would see all those signs but still didn't believe that I was worthy of such happiness. So, I decided to share my thoughts with Vania. Perhaps she could pray with me and God could talk to her as well. That way, I could confirm if what I wanted to do was His will—if it was really coming from Him, and not my will—or coming from my human nature.

As soon as I started telling Vania about the Pan Am games, Frank, and Canada, she interrupted me.

"So, have you got your bags packed yet?" She gave me a big smile, then picked up her laptop computer. Together, we browsed a lot of images on the Internet of the most beautiful places in Vancouver. She began to ask me to describe what I would do when visiting each of these places. We spent hours dreaming and laughing together, and when I left her house, I was in peace. All that I needed to know was that God would be with me no matter where, under any circumstances. That night, and throughout the following days, He kept sending signs that yes, He would.

So, I took courage and sent my documents, together with the visitor visa request form to Canadian Immigration. Even before they sent the response, I started to donate most of my furniture, books, clothing, and stuff that I couldn't take with me. By that time, I knew, deep in my heart, that I was never meant to spend all my life in Brazil. This trip was just the starting point. As Vania used to say, "I was born to fly high, like the eagles."

I prayed a lot; I was always asking for guidance and wisdom. One day, when I was in prayer, I felt the Holy Spirit guiding me not to tell anyone about my plans. At church, I learned that when we are about to do something great, which will bring glory to God, the enemy gets really upset and tries to sabotage our plans, sometimes using someone close to us. So, I kept my plans secret as much as I could and asked the Lord to show me the right time to tell my mother and siblings about the trip. He does know everything and we should trust Him every day more and more. My mom reacted very badly to the news.

"What? You're going to leave behind a secure, stable government job?" she yelled. "You know how hard those are to get. That's totally irresponsible, from anyone's point of view."

She tried to bring me "back to my senses" in her own particular way, by yelling and offending, using harsh words, but I was in peace. Yes, I knew it was crazy, but I also knew that this was what I was meant to do. So, I kept quiet and let her express her opinion. Then, when I felt it was the appropriate moment, I got up from her old couch, looked into her eyes, and spoke with a calm and firm voice, just like someone who knew exactly what she was doing.

"I'm not here asking for permission," I told her. "I'm telling you my decision. The only thing that's up to you is whether we're on good terms when I leave."

Quietly, my mom got up from her couch and started to walk towards the garage. I followed her, in silence, not understanding what she was trying to do. When she entered her car, she locked herself inside, turned on the engine, and drove out of her house, without telling me where she was going, I realized that by pretending she needed to go somewhere, she was trying to avoid a bigger conflict.

For almost a week, she didn't talk to me at all, but I kept visiting her every day. She would ignore me and I would ignore her ignoring me. It was funny. It seemed like a joke and I was sure she was enjoying that. But when I got my visa approved, she realized that it was real: I was going to Canada, and nothing she could do would change that.

So, my mother began to talk to me again. Not only that, but she started to defend me when our relatives found out about my trip and started to question my sanity. She also bought me a nice winter jacket for Christmas. She asked me to spend my last night in Brazil at her place together as a family: me, my little sister, baby brother (even though he is now twenty-five, he will always be my baby brother), and her.

After the Christmas season was over, the days seemed to pass a lot faster than I expected. I booked my flight for January 19. I still had a lot of things to organize, furniture that I couldn't find someone to take, and a lot of paperwork. I didn't want to resign yet from work; human nature convinced me to keep it as a backup plan, so I took vacation time instead. I wanted to visit some friends and go through a medical checkup, just to make sure I would not need to visit a doctor while I was in Vancouver.

Meanwhile, Frank went to Hungary to spend some time with old friends and relatives. He would be arriving in Vancouver just a week before me. While he was in Europe, we were using social media to keep in touch, so our relationship became public to everyone, including one of his ex-girlfriends. Let's call her Barbara. She used to work at the same gymnasium as Frank and his parents did in Richmond, BC. Therefore, even though they were no longer together, because of their proximity, she had maintained the hope that at any time, he would agree to start dating her again.

Well, my presence in Vancouver would definitely change her chances. So, she began to spread lies about us to all of his friends and to the parents of his athletes. One time, she also found my telephone number and called me.

"You know, I feel sorry for you," she said, "because Frank and I are still together. In fact, when you guys met, we were just upset with each other."

"That's not true!" I was on a bus commuting from work to my place. She had caught me by surprise. I got so nervous, I started shaking.

"We never actually broke up, you know."

"I can't believe you have the nerve to tell me such lies," I replied.

"If you stay with him, he'll dump you when you get to Canada."

"He's told me about you two. I know that you're through."

I felt so embarrassed, even though almost no one on the bus would understand what we were saying in English. Yet, I felt as if every passenger knew exactly what was going on.

"No way. To Frank, you were just a temporary fling. I'm not going to let you ruin my life and career. For your own sake, you should stay in Brazil and forget about coming to Vancouver. Whatever Frank told you, it was a lie."

"Well, I'm sorry and I promise to take care of the situation."

"Good, because otherwise, you'll be sorry."

Although she had caught me off guard, I couldn't help but notice that she kept repeating words like "my work, my career and my future" while bad-mouthing him. She was definitely talking about someone I had never met, about a man who, according to her, was crazy and had a very bad attitude. I heard all that she had to say. Not for a moment did she sound like someone fighting for love. I just wanted her to hang up so that I could process this out-of-the-blue information. It was clear I needed to confront Frank, but something inside of me told me to calm down and be still. I can only believe it was the Holy Spirit guiding me because that would never have come from me; to be still was not something that I knew how to do best. To keep me from jumping to conclusions and calling him right way, I began to pray nonstop until I finally arrived at home.

A lot calmer, I decided to go visit Vania and ask her for help. Then I had a moment of sudden realization. Remember Marisa, the woman I had met in Fortaleza four years before? Vania had told me that I should learn something from her. (An ex-girlfriend of Marisa's boyfriend had kept calling and texting her, saying lies about she and him still seeing each other; Marisa had given up and let him go.) I was covered in goose bumps. When I had met Marisa, I was proud to think that I was teaching her about not giving up, but God knew ahead of time that years later, I would face the same situation she did. When He crossed our paths, he was preparing me for this moment. I didn't want the same result as Marisa. Her experience taught me that the only one way I could change the end of my own story was by conquering fear and not giving up.

After that insight moment, I went to visit Vania, but no longer to ask her for help. Instead, I went there to share what God had just revealed to me and how amazing it was. What a beautiful thing He did for me! From her house, I had the opportunity to talk to Frank and tell him what Barbara had said.

"I'm sorry you had to talk to her," he told me. "She must have found your number on my phone. I leave it in the office when I'm at work in the gym. Please don't believe a word she said. She is just trying to ruin my life."

Relief swept through me.

"I want to remind you, sweetie," Frank continued, "that you've met all of my family members and friends through Skype, my parents and sister wrote you emails with Merry Christmas wishes, and said how they're looking forward to meeting you," he said. "If Barbara was telling the truth, that would make my whole family liars, right?".

"You're right."

I laughed, reassured by his logic and support. I was so glad that I didn't call him right after Barbara had hung up. I would have missed the best that God had prepared for me. Since the day she called and we spoke on the phone, I never talked to her again. She kept texting me but I never answered. One day, as the texts stopped coming, I understood what the Bible meant when it says that God will fight our battles on our behalf: *"The Lord will fight for you, and you shall hold your peace"* (Exodus 14:14 (NKJV)).

I was obedient, and as hard as it was to calm down and be still, it was worth it. I passed through this trial. The big day had arrived; in less than twenty-four hours, I would be travelling outside the country for the first time, to a place where I knew only a few people and just enough of their language to survive. I had packed all my belongings in two suit cases, one regular-sized, weighing 24 kg, and one carry-on, weighing no more than 7 kg. After so many signs, I realized that I should trust in God to provide for all my needs; therefore, I took only the essentials with me.

I had given away everything else except an old wardrobe that nobody had shown interest in. Because it was in perfect condition, I didn't want to throw it away. I asked my mother to take it as she had a spare room in her house. She told me she didn't need it but agreed to help me if I would deliver it, unassembled, to her house.

I didn't have much cash on me; I had exchanged almost all that I had into Canadian dollars. So, it was difficult to find a company that would do the work for the amount that I was able to pay. I was getting so frustrated that I started contemplating the garbage option. But then I called a number in the Yellow Pages that I hadn't tried yet. This was my last resort. I began to pray. The person on the other side of the line answered with such warmth that I felt compelled to share my entire situation. The voice belonged to a nice old man who felt compassion for me. He decided to help me even though the amount of money I had wasn't enough to pay for that kind of service.

He delivered the wardrobe parts to my mother's garage, as promised, and wished me good luck. He gave me his business card in case someone from my family needed his services again. I took the card in my hands and silently read the words: "EASY MOVE— Because when God wants, it is like that!" Amen.

Chapter 11

Canada Smells like Coffee

"Open to me the gates of righteousness; I will go through them, And I will praise the Lord."

Psalm 118:19 (NKJV)

ON THE MORNING OF MY TRIP to Canada, I woke up very excited. Finally, the day had arrived. In a few hours, I would be with Frank. The two months we had spent apart seemed like a whole year. I missed him so much, but my excitement also had to do with the fact that I was leaving the country for the first time, like I had always dreamed. After many years of hearing people around me say that I would never be able to do something like that, I ended up believing in those lies. But that was about to change. I was about to write a new story and oh yeah, I was more than ready. I was prepared and well trained.

If you go back and review all that I have told you until now, you will agree that I was trained by God to take this big step without fear.

Dora, my former roommate, came to my mom's house to say goodbye since she couldn't go to the airport. She spent some time with me and helped me finish packing a few things that I had left for the last minute. We hugged and cried a lot. We had gone through so many things in such a short period of time; we would certainly miss each other's company. Saying goodbye to a good friend like Dora is never easy.

Later that day, my mother, my siblings, and I had lunch together—our last one as a family before I left Brazil. We had a great time. We laughed and enjoyed every second of those few hours that we still had. Then the schoolhouse clock on our kitchen door reminded us that it was time to go. We had to be at the airport two hours before departure.

When we all got there, Vania and her husband were already waiting. They said they couldn't let me go without their blessings; they loved me and wanted to see, with their own eyes, my dream becoming reality. I never imagined that it would be so painful to pass through security and not be able to see my mom, Lili, and Marcelo, or my friends. I couldn't hold back my tears. As much as I was happy for the life waiting for me, I was sad for the life I was leaving behind. Yes, it was a hard life; many times, I thought it was unfair, but it was everything that I had, all that I knew, who I was. Believe me, it wasn't easy to wave goodbye one last time and get onto the plane, but I did.

As I entered that plane, I also entered into a new series of thoughts, no longer about my past, but about my present situation. I was travelling alone and would remain like that, all by myself, for the next twenty-two hours. I would have to change planes two times, first in Sao Paulo (Brazil) and then in Toronto (Canada), where I would have to go through Customs and Immigration. I had never had to change planes before; on all previous times, I had a direct flight. Both airports were really big and busy, (at least a lot more than all the others I'd been to). But the most terrifying thought had to do with the stories of people sent back home by Customs and Immigration, even though they had valid documents, just because they couldn't explain well enough the purpose of their trip. When I thought about that, fear started to fill my heart and almost paralyzed me. But it was already too late to give up, even more so because people were behind me, pushing me forward, trying to find their seats. There was no turning back. So, I drew on all the strength I had left and started to walk towards my place, praying to have at least a comfortable chair, by the aisle.

I am positive that God wanted to make that trip something special, to be shared with others. I say that because I experienced several miracles from the moment I stepped into that first plane until I arrived in Vancouver, starting with that aisle seat I had requested. A crisply dressed, thirtyish couple sitting beside me were going to Sao Paulo for business. They noticed I was carrying a pink pillow in the shape of a dog.

"That's really cute," said the woman. "Where did you buy it? Are there any left?"

I told them the story behind my pillow. I had wanted to buy something that my sister could keep as a token of my love for her, something to remind her of all the things we have in common. At her favourite craft fair, I bought the only two dogs left. They were siblings, just like us, who would have to be apart from each other, but would always stay connected by the love shared between each other. The couple loved the story.

After that, we talked about many other things until our flight reached the airport in Sao Paulo, where I was supposed to have a five-hour layover. But we got there one hour later than expected. When I finally passed through security, they had already started with the boarding. It all happened so fast, I had to run from place to place. The staff at the airport was anything but helpful. I remember thanking God that I was still in Brazil, where people speak Portuguese, allowing me to understand what they were saying, even when they were mumbling.

I had promised my family and Frank that I would call, letting them know where and how was I throughout the trip. But for some reason, my cell phone didn't work there and I had no time to stop by a phone booth. So, I left Sao Paulo without talking to any of them, hoping that from Toronto I would be able call and explain what had happened.

The second plane was huge. Until that day, I had never seen so many seats, and they were all occupied. I was amazed. My ticket was for coach class, but I had a large chair, blanket, and touch-screen TV. Today, I take these things for granted, but at that time, I appreciated them so much, I thought I was flying first class. I was so happy, that I even felt bad asking God to have me sit by the aisle again. That was why I didn't mind when I got to my seat and found out that it was in the middle.

As I said before, the Lord wanted to make this trip something remarkable, an experience above and beyond anything I could ever imagine. To do that, he sent me two Canadian angels; I am going to call them Zara and Greg.

They were a twenty-something couple returning to Canada from their honeymoon in Brazil. They were supposed to sit apart from each other: one by the window and the other by the aisle. I was supposed to sit between them, but Zara asked me to change places so that they could be together.

Of course, I said yes, resulting not only in a spacious seat by the aisle (as I had always wanted), but in a very pleasant trip as well. Between naps, we spent the next ten hours talking about all kinds of stuff, how they enjoyed their time in Brazil and the places they visited, about my plans for sightseeing in Vancouver, and how Frank and I had met. We exchanged emails and promised to keep in touch.

Although everything was going better than expected, my human nature would always bring me back to a place of worry and doubt. I was so nervous about the possible questions I would have to answer at Customs and Immigration, about my luggage and how I would find it or how to find the gate for my next flight, that I could barely sleep. Even though I was tired, I would close my eyes but minutes later, I was wake. My brain was super active. Those thoughts were so overwhelming that I was about to burst into tears. Then, inside of me, I heard: "Just ask and the door will be open." I recognized that verse. It was from the Bible, Matthew 7:7-8: *"Ask, and it will be given to you; seek, and you will find; knock, and it will be opened to you. For everyone who asks receives, and he who seeks finds, and to him who knocks it will be opened."*

So, I decided to pray, and ask God to open the doors of Canada to me. Finally, after some time praying, I found rest and fell asleep. Then, I woke up with the sign Fasten Your Seatbelt activated. We were about to land in Toronto. I turned to my left side and there was Zara, smiling.

"Are you excited?" she asked me.

"Yes, but I have no clue what to do next."

"Just follow me and Greg. We'll help you get to your gate." They helped me to look for my bags and filed a claim for me, because one of them was missing. After that, Greg went to grab us some coffee while Zara walked me to my gate. He would meet us there. But because of my missing luggage and the time spent putting in a claim for it, when we got to the gate, they were already boarding passengers. Once again, I couldn't call my family or Frank. Nor could I wait for Greg to thank him for all of his help. But I did have time to hug Zara one more time and we took a picture together.

Inside of the plane, I recognized a Brazilian woman I had met when complaining about my belongings. She, too, had had problems with her luggage and my new friends had helped her as well. She was seated right in front of me, beside some strange, but very nice man, who agreed to switch places with me so that she and I could sit together. She asked me if I could sit by the aisle, in her place, because she preferred the window. I couldn't be happier about that.

I took a moment to thank God for that amazing trip. For not even a minute was I alone throughout the whole experience. He put some nice people on my side to help me and to keep me company. Even though I couldn't request beforehand, I had my preferable seat on every flight. Things couldn't be better than that—at least that was what I thought. Right then, I heard the flight attendant calling my name; she had looked for me in my original seat and couldn't find me. I lifted my hand, and she walked towards me with a cup of coffee from a famous Canadian coffee company.

"Your friends, Zara and Greg, asked me to deliver to you your first cup of coffee on Canadian land," she said. "Welcome to Canada, Sabrina!".

My heart was almost jumping out of my throat. Only one thing could beat such a joyful moment, and that would be looking into Frank's big blue eyes while running to him and throwing myself into his arms. At that moment, I would smell his cologne again, the one that was already fading away from the shirt he gave me so that I could remember him. I used to sleep with it close to my face. And I would kiss him again, and feel the same emotion that I felt when we had first kissed.

I did run into his arms and I did feel all that, but it wasn't as romantic as I had imagined. But remember: God's works are perfect. He knows everything we will need before we even ask. Because I couldn't call either my family or Frank since I had left Aracaju, and they were without news for almost twenty-four hours, my sister Lili decided to call Frank and asked him if I had arrived. Since we were little, Lili and I have had very similar voices; it was difficult for anybody, including our mother, to distinguish who was talking. In addition to that, my sister's English wasn't that great at the time, so when she called him, instead of saying: "Is Sabrina there?" she said: "Sabrina is here?"

They didn't understand each other. After that, my family started to worry a lot more. Even worse than that, Frank began to think that I was the one on the phone, telling him that I was in Brazil. He thought I had given up and started to question whether he should go to the airport or not.

When I arrived in Vancouver, I looked around and saw nobody familiar at all. I began to think that Frank had given up. But before I had time to freak out, I heard someone calling my name through the loudspeakers. I approached security, saying that I was the person they were looking for. They asked me to provide them with an address where my missing luggage should be delivered.

I had Frank's address written in my daytimer, but didn't even know if Frank would show up. If he didn't, I would have to go to a hotel, but I didn't know which one. I was so confused and embarrassed.

"I'm sorry, but I can't give you an answer just yet," I said to the surprised man behind the counter. "Just give me a minute. I'll call my boyfriend, find out what's going on, and then I can give you an address."

The Brazilian cellphone company that I had a contract with didn't offer any kind of service in Vancouver, even though, back in Brazil, they had said it would work just fine. I couldn't believe what I was going through. With tears in my eyes, I looked at the Brazilian woman and asked her to lend me her phone so that I could call Frank and find out what my immediate future would look like. She handed her phone to me and I called him.

"I'm here, I'm here, at the airport in Vancouver," he said. "Where are you?"

"I'm in Vancouver too. I'm at the airport."

He was thrilled. After my sister had called, even though he had had doubts, he had thought about all the things that we had gone through since we met. He decided to show up anyway.

"I wanted to prove to myself that I had done everything in my power to make this relationship work."

His reassuring words made me feel secure. Even though I knew Frank would take good care of me during my stay in Canada, it was good to hear this. But with all of the confusion my sister had created and the avalanche of doubting thoughts in his head, Frank forgot that I was coming through domestic arrivals. So, he was waiting for me at the international arrival area. I offer thanks to God, who put that Brazilian woman on my path, so that I could call him just before he gave up waiting.

I did run to Frank's arms, but what I first felt was more like relief than any other emotion. It was a really scary situation and took me some time to calm down. But after he finished giving his address to the airline agent and we said goodbye to the Brazilian woman who saved my day, we left the airport holding hands. It was just like when we used to walk on the beach in Aracaju. I felt something much better than what I had hoped for: I felt God's presence.

The only thing I still don't remember from that trip is if I passed through Customs and Immigration or not. I know that I must have, but it didn't seem like it. The only thing I remember is that I gave my passport to a nice man who was smiling. He looked into my eyes, put a stamp on it, and gave it back to me.

"Have a very good day," he said.

Isn't God amazing? He not only listened to my prayers and opened the doors of Canada to me, but planned my entire trip. He put all those people, at the right place, at the right time to help me to fulfill my destiny.

Chapter 12

New Land, New Challenges, Same God

"Many are the afflictions of the righteous, but the Lord delivers him out of them all."

Psalm 34:19 (NKJV)

AS SOON AS FRANK AND I left the airport, I asked him to drive me to a small Catholic church nearby. I had found its address on the Internet when I was still in Brazil, when planning the trip. I wanted to make sure that the first place I visited would be the House of the Lord, so that I could worship and thank him for all that he had done and to ask for his protection as I was entering a new stage in my life.

As we started driving, I called my family and Vania to let them know that I was fine. It felt good hearing their voices but it felt even better when we parked at the church. We arrived at the church very quickly. It was a beautiful sunny day; there were no clouds in the sky. It was so perfect I couldn't help but think how amazing it would be if Vania could see, with my eyes, all those yellow and red flowers in the garden, the buildings, and the church, which was open but empty.

I went in and Frank followed me. I knew he wasn't a Christian; Frank did not even believe in God, but I was at peace with that. After so many signs and prayers, I knew deep in my heart that God was present in our relationship; he wanted us to be together. Frank probably felt uncomfortable when I knelt on the floor and began to pray, but I didn't care. I did it anyway because I thought that it would be a great opportunity for him to know with whom he was about to live.

After I was done with prayer, we left the church and he drove me to his parents' house, where they were expecting us to have lunch together. He didn't say a word about what he saw at the church. As I mentioned before, Frank was a very respectful man, and the fact that we didn't share the same beliefs didn't bother him, at least for a while.

I knew his parents and sister from our talks over the computer, but we never had time to get to have a meaningful conversation. As I met them in person, I realized that they were a lot nicer than I thought. In the following days, since Frank was busy working as a full-time men's head coach in Richmond, BC, he dropped me off at his parents' place so that I would have company. His sister and her husband took me sightseeing to a lot of places. So did his parents. We spent a long time together. Their Hungarian culture was very different from Canada's or Brazil's and that wasn't a big deal in the beginning.

But as we got to know each other better, the conflicts started. Like Frank, they didn't believe in God, church, charity or any kind of deed unless it had a lucrative purpose. So, it was very difficult for them to understand why I started a volunteer job at a Christian fair trade organization. I understood that they meant well. They felt responsible for me since my family wasn't around, and they didn't want people taking advantage of me. But I knew what I was doing, so I put my foot down and kept working there, which made them very unhappy.

As a visitor, I was not allowed to attend any kind of school or start paid labour. So, I had to spend most days at home by myself or watch Frank coaching his athletes, which later became very boring. Volunteering at that store helped me to get out of the house and kept me busy. I was able to learn about Canadian culture, improve my English, and to make some friends.

Frank was a good man and he was trying to accommodate my needs as much as he could, but that didn't keep us from having several arguments. Most of the time, I was the one starting the fight. Before I came to Canada, Frank promised me that he would stop smoking cigarettes. I truly believed that it was something easy for him to do, that it was just a bad habit, that it was all about him making a choice. "If he only he'd try harder," I used to think. But believe me, he did try. He would quit for a week or two and then a friend would invite him to go out for a smoke and he would start smoking again.

I lost count of how many times we fought over that. I was so focused on helping him get rid of that addiction that I didn't realize I was becoming a horrible person. He would come home from work with a smile on his face, ready to give me a kiss, and I would stop him halfway to smell his neck or hands, looking for evidence that he had smoked.

To avoid conflict, Frank started lying to me. He would park his car somewhere to smoke and after he finished, he would wash his hands and use deodorant spray. Then he would come home late, smelling good, telling me that traffic was bad or that he needed to stop to go to a bathroom. Well, that didn't work. It only made things worse, because I began to think that he was cheating on me. Feeling insecure, I started to question our relationship and spent days wondering if I had done something wrong.

After struggling for a while, I was so depressed that I quit my work as a volunteer. I didn't want to leave home or hear people say that I should go back to Brazil. I really loved Frank. The thought of living without him was even worse than remaining in that situation. I kept praying and asking God for help. I used to wait for Frank to go to work and then I would go to church and cry for hours. One time, I called the priest and asked him for help. I didn't tell him that I was once married because I knew what the Bible says about divorce. But I did tell him what was bothering me.

"What you need is a group of friends," he said. I had met one woman at the fair trade organization while I was still helping them, but she was always busy between work, volunteering, and helping her family. I also knew the physiotherapist who travelled with the Canadian team to Brazil, but she lived one-and-a-half hours away. She, too, had a very busy schedule.

Trying to assist me, the priest introduced me to a nice woman who was originally from the Philippines and had moved to Canada when she was still very young. She was very active and loved to host parties and play sports. She invited me to some events and after some time, we became very good friends.

Then, Frank had to leave me alone in Vancouver, for the first time, as he travelled to Australia for ten days for a competition. It was, by far, the hardest moment of my life since I had landed in Canada three months earlier. In Australia, he was nineteen hours ahead of me. As much as he tried to keep in touch, I couldn't help but think that he was avoiding me. I was so insecure that one night, I woke up from a nightmare in which Frank was cheating on me. I tried to call him but his phone was off the hook. I almost died of anxiety. I called Vania and asked her to go to the computer because I needed to see her. My entire body was shaking and I couldn't control my thoughts. Vania helped me to remember that God was with me. She reminded me that based on past experiences, I should already know that from those hard times something good always comes. It was really good that Vania and I had kept our friendship, even though we were so far from each other. After almost two hours of talking, I finally calmed down.

Frank called me on my phone. We talked a lot. I was so mad at him that I did not even make a big deal when he told me that with the distance between us, he had come to understand how much he loved me.

"I want to be with you forever," he said. His words hardly registered. Could I take them seriously? Maybe I was just going to get hurt all over again.

"I think we should get married this summer, when my grandma is visiting from Hungary."

I was so blinded by fear and jealously that I didn't give too much credit to what he was saying. I thought he was just saying this to get out of the fight I had started over the phone. But I did hear what he said. The following Sunday, after church, when my female friend asked me how things were going between Frank and me, I told her what he had said. She did what I should have done: gone crazy with joy and applause. Immediately, she opened her daytimer and started playing with the pages. After some time, she stopped on July 24 and wrote down: "Sabrina and Frank's Wedding Party." Then she looked at me, smiled, and said: "I already set the date for you."

Frank came back to Canada a few weeks before his twenty-ninth birthday in June. That meant that if we were indeed getting married that summer, we had less than two months to organize everything. But I didn't do anything. I was still expecting a formal proposal and was too proud to ask him if he really meant what he said. Frank, on the other hand, didn't want to bring that up again. He was more concerned about my request to extend my visitor visa; would it be accepted or not? Otherwise, we would be getting married and then would both have to move to Brazil or else he would end up living in Canada alone. So, we kept living like we had never talked about marriage until the day of his birthday.

We went out to celebrate. Halfway back to our home, he received a text message from one of the coaches he had met in Australia. She had sent him her picture as a birthday gift and wrote "so you can always remember that you have a friend on the other side of the world." In my insanity, that message was proof, a sign, that my nightmare was, in fact, true: Frank had, indeed, cheated on me, and that was the woman.

I soon learned that Frank had never met this woman outside the gym where the competition was going on. She had asked for his phone number and that of two other coaches representing Canada in Australia because she was looking for an opportunity to work abroad; she wanted to use their names as referrals. Thanks to social media, when she saw it was Frank's birthday, she thought it would be okay to send him her photo; Frank did not appreciate this.

I was so insecure, I had a hard time believing him. I was determined to leave Frank. As soon as we got home, I began to pack my belongings. I had it all figured out: I would spend the night at my friend's house, the one from my volunteer work, and in the morning, I would ask my other friend, the physiotherapist, to take me to the airport. It's amazing what fear can do to us; I had completely lost my reasoning. For those horrible hours we were fighting over that picture, I acted as if I had also lost my faith in God.

Then Frank did something that nobody had ever done to me before: he locked the apartment door and put the key inside his pocket. He hid my luggage and started to cry.

"Why did you do that?" I yelled at him while scrambling to try and find my bags.

"Because I don't want to see you leave," he said, weakly, while sobbing.

I had spent twenty-eight years of my life hearing people asking me to leave. This was the first time someone wanted me to stay. Frank was ready to fight a lot more to have me with him, but he didn't need to. After hearing those words, something changed inside me. I regained my senses and decided not only to stay, but also to look for help.

I felt the desire to confess my sins to someone, but refused to believe that this was an answer to my prayers. These conflicting thoughts didn't make any sense to me.

When I became a follower of Christ, I repented my sins and had shared that with Vania and some people from our church group. So, at that moment, it seemed like just a silly thing to do. But as the days passed, that feeling didn't go away. It became stronger and stronger. All the passages in Bible that I put my eyes on were about confessing sins. I felt like if I didn't talk, the words would jump out of my mouth, along with my heart.

One day, overwhelmed by that feeling, I looked for an open church where I could find a priest at the confessional. It wasn't easy. I went from church to church. When I did find one, the priest said he couldn't hear my confession because I was divorced and living with another man. Since then, I have never again gone back to a Catholic church. I have much respect for all of my Catholic friends and family members and I truly believe that they are people of God. But I was entering a season in my life in which I wanted to be around people who were fighting to have me with them instead of pushing me away and asking me to leave. It was wrong, I know now. I shouldn't have been living with a man before marriage, but I was looking for help. I thought the priest could have granted me a little mercy. Perhaps, after that, he could have persuaded me to do what was right.

Instead, he sent me away, refusing to learn about my worries, let alone my sins.

But I still needed to confess. After that incident with the priest, the desire became a lot stronger. One day, I drove to an evangelical free church close to my home and asked the receptionist to help me. She took me to the minister's office and asked me: "Would you like a cup of tea or coffee while you wait for the pastor?"

Was I the only one who noticed a huge difference from the start, compared to the Catholic church? The pastor came in and to my surprise, it was a woman. She was nice and sweet. She heard me without judgement and helped me figure out what was bothering me so much, why it was hard for me to trust in Frank. Yes, I had accepted the decision to come to Canada because I believed that God was giving me an opportunity to be happy and loved. But deep inside, I still didn't believe I deserved that happiness or love. Because of that, I thought that some time, soon, that opportunity would be taken away from me.

I realized that she was right. I repented and asked for forgiveness. We prayed and I went home. I kept praying persistently, asking God to remove fear from my heart, and to help me trust more not only in Frank, but mostly in Him. I asked the Lord to remind me why I came to Canada and to help me to fulfill my dreams.

A couple days later, I received a letter from the Government of Canada, approving my request to extend my stay for another six months.

Chapter 13

They Need To Know and We Must Say It

"I have come as a light into the world, that whoever believes in Me should not abide in darkness."

John 12:46 (NKJV)

DURING MY FIRST DAYS IN CANADA, I got very upset with Frank's father. He has this particular way of saying what he thinks which, sometimes, sounds very much like sarcasm. For instance, when someone broke into our car and stole my camera from the glove compartment, he wanted to tell me that it wasn't wise to leave expensive items in the car. Instead, he joked about the high crime rate in Brazil and asked me: "Would you leave things like that inside your car in Brazil?"

Those who know him well know that he has a huge heart and would never say a word to hurt anybody. But his jokes can sound truly hurtful to someone who doesn't know what he really means. Since I grew up hearing my mother saying a lot of hurtful things, I didn't want to go over all that again.

"I don't appreciate these kind of jokes," I told him. "I don't think this is the way to teach me anything."

He thought I was being disrespectful but didn't say a word. For several days, he stopped talking to me, waiting for me to apologize. But in my eyes, he should have been the one apologizing. Tired of being in the middle of this pickle, Frank asked me, "Can you not just consider saying you're sorry for your behaviour, even if you don't mean it?

"Sorry, but I'm not willing to do that," I replied. "If I say something to him, I have to believe in what I'm saying."

So, I had to ask help from God. I prayed for wisdom and asked Jesus to soften the heart of Frank's father to receive what I was going to say. I also asked Him to help me to find the right words and the right time to talk.

As the days passed, I felt like I would never have the courage to take the blame for something I hadn't done. But one morning, Frank told me he needed to leave home a little earlier so he could stop by his parents to fix their computer before going to work. When I heard him say that, I instantly felt something burning inside of me. My heart was pumping so fast, I could barely breathe. I recognized that feeling, having experienced it a few times; I have learned to be obedient to God and follow the instructions that usually come with that overwhelming sensation.

"Wait for me," I told Frank. "I'm getting dressed because I'm ready to talk to your father."

When we arrived at his parents' place, it was like they were expecting me. Frank's mother gave me a kiss and left the room. Frank went to their home office while his father stayed exactly where he was when I entered the house: sitting at the dining room table. He avoided looking me in the eye, but seemed ready to listen. So, I took a deep breath and let the Holy Spirit talk.

"For how long will you keep ignoring me?", I asked.

No answer.

So I continued: "You know... We don't have to agree on everything to live in harmony. We just need respect each other. I look up to you. Is that how you want me to behave every time we have a disagreement?"

He nodded.

"So, come on here and give me a hug!", I said.

We never had a problem again. We became so close, that now, when he wants a second opinion about something important, he usually asks me. I earned his respect not by power, not by knowledge, but through prayer and obedience to God. After all, Jesus said to turn the other cheek. I'm telling you this because with that experience, I learned that we are each the light in the world. If we want to see a transformation, we must be the good example. When I humbled myself before Frank's father, God exalted me.

Happy with the outcome, I went home and Frank went to work. I needed to tell somebody about what had just happened to me, but I was alone. I decided to go for a walk in the park near our apartment. I took an old block of paper and a pen, sat down on the grass, and wrote a letter to the Lord, just as if I was writing to a best friend, telling Him about the news.

I was so distracted with my writings that I jumped up, scared, when a seventyish-looking man dressed in a black suit on a hot day stopped in front of me. He walked and talked slowly, but seemed very wise. Extending a hand, he gave me a little book. It was the New Testament. We talked for a few minutes, only enough time for him to give me the address of his church. But before he said goodbye, he said something that stirred a fire inside my heart, something that helped me move to a next phase of my life in this new land.

"Never forget what you are supposed to do here, in Canada," he told me. Then he left. If I had not kept a record of that conversation, or the book he gave me, I would probably think it was just a dream. Sometimes, even for Christians like me, who have just experienced the goodness of God only a few hours before, such a thing could not be real. That man didn't know me, and yet, he said exactly what I needed to hear to make a major change in my life.

When I was still in Brazil, getting ready to come to Canada, my friend Denia told me I would be the one to bring Jesus to Frank and his family. But I was so scared to force my faith on them and drive them away. Until that day, I had never talked to Frank about God or His goodness. I kept my faith so private it almost seemed like a secret. On Sundays, I would leave for church early in the morning and come back before Frank even woke up. During the week, I would pray or listen to worship songs when he was not around.

That stranger in the black suit gave me my first Gospel in English. His actions and words inspired me to be bold and approach Frank. Since he was no stranger, that should be even easier, I thought. The stranger had reminded me: "Trust in the Holy Spirit to give you the right words and opportunities."

If I wanted to catch Frank's attention to listen me talking about God, I would need to make it sound appealing. Knowing that he has a passion for sports, I decided I should start, somehow, from there. So, I ran back home and sat in front of the computer for the rest of the afternoon. Researching examples of Christian athletes, I found many with successful careers; I was planning to show them to Frank "unintentionally." Then I saw a trailer for an old Christian movie called *Facing the Giants*, the one I had watched, years ago, in Brazil during the entrance exams for the public university. Since it was a great movie about the relationship between a coach and his athletes, I thought it would be an excellent way to start. And I was right. That night, Frank and I watched the movie and that was how it all started: he began to look at me and my faith a lot differently.

The following day, it was beautiful outside: sunny and warm with a blue, cloudless sky. Frank took me with him to the gym. Between training his athletes, he would have a two-hour break and planned to spend it with me, watching the ducks, geese, and other birds at the Richmond Nature Park. Before his first training started, Frank spent some time talking to his parents about the movie. They didn't like the idea of watching it because it was Christian based.

"Watch it like I did," he told them. "Just focus on what's interesting for you: the sports angle." Hearing that made me wonder if he had missed the most important message: God is real. He is alive and is willing to help whoever asks for help, even with the most impossible things.

As planned, Frank and I went for our walk in the park. We watched some cute little birds and a couple of ducks walk clumsily amidst a beautiful family of Canada geese heading towards a little pond. Two big owls flew around us, looping in the air; we could see them diving to the ground to catch a rat. We had a lot of fun, but I accidentally locked the car keys inside our vehicle. The spare keys were at home and Frank needed to go back to work in less than twenty minutes. When he called the insurance company, a representative told him that this was not covered in his plan; but if he wanted, he could renew before the expiration date and add the coverage for an extra amount. Only after that could they send someone to help him. It would take at least forty minutes.

While Frank was talking on the phone, I was praying, asking God to help us get Frank to work on time. He was still on the phone when a locksmithing van stopped right beside our car. Not knowing what was going on between Frank and the insurance company, I approached the driver.

"Are you here to help us?" I asked him.

"A customer called me but when I got here, nobody was around except you two." We didn't know who had called for the van, but it certainly was an angel. Only by God's grace did that man show up where we were, when we needed him, available to give us a hand. For a smaller amount of money than what the insurance company wanted to charge, the nice man opened our car's door fast enough to get us to the gym just in time for the second training. I witnessed another miracle: for the first time, I heard Frank thanking God for His help.

"I guess I should thank God for that?" he asked me.

"I believe God is already saying 'Any time, son'," I replied. My smile would have gone around my head if my ears weren't in the way.

That same night, we went home, talking about the movie and our experience at the park. He asked me how faith works and I told him everything I knew and what I believed. At home, I caught him fiddling with my Bible. I stood quietly, behind the bedroom door, watching him look at it like a child, so curious and full of questions. I didn't say a word; firstly, because I didn't want to overwhelm him, and secondly, because I had learned something very important: there is a time to be quiet and a time to talk. As a follower of Christ, it's crucial not only to identify those times, but to act accordingly, even when it seems too hard or too weird.

Chapter 14

We All Have Skeletons in the Closet

"And you shall know the truth, and the truth shall make you free."

John 8:32 (NKJV)

ONCE MY VISITOR VISA was extended for six months, Frank and I decided we should get married in July, during his vacation. This way, we could apply for my work visa and permanent resident status from inside the country, and I would not need to leave until a decision was made.

But before planning anything, I was still expecting a formal marriage proposal from Frank. One morning in mid-June, he was reading some emails on his phone while inside the washroom in our master bedroom suite. I was lying on our bed, reading a book, waiting for him to come out so that we could have lunch together. Suddenly, he slid open the washroom door a little less than halfway, just enough so I could hear, but not see him.

"Can we set our wedding date for the same day as my grandma's birthday?" he asked me.

I was stunned. No ring, no flowers, no kneeling on the floor.

"Yes," I said.

That was it. But God knew I had always dreamed of something memorable and perfect.

"When's your grandma's birthday?" I asked him.

"July 24." I almost passed out. All the magic and excitement that we, women, expect in a proposal, came in that moment, when I realized that a month before, my friend from church had already "set" that day as "our date" when Frank was still in Australia. It's amazing how we can sometimes completely ignore these little signs. Many people think they are coincidence, but when we walk in prayer, we know and feel, deep in our hearts, that they are a divine providence.

Having established the desired date, we had only about forty days to announce the news to our friends and families, get a marriage licence, book the wedding officiant, find a venue, and get me a dress. Even though we knew we didn't have enough time, we decided not to hurry with the arrangements. We took one step at a time.

First, we needed to announce the engagement to our family and close friends. I felt more apprehensive about how my parents-in-law would respond to the news than how my mother would react after finding out that I would not be moving back to Brazil. Even though I knew they liked me, I was not Hungarian. I always had the impression that because of their language and culture, they wished that Frank would find a Hungarian bride. So, I prayed for a whole week, asking God to open their hearts to accept me, as one of them, into their family. On Saturday that same week, Frank took me to the gym with him. With me at his side, he told his parents: "We want to get married at the end of the month."

Their eyes filled with joy; their faces looked even brighter than usual. Frank's dad gave his son a long hug, then kept tapping his shoulder, saying: "Well done, my son." They didn't ask, but Frank explained the reason for our hurry. They understood that it was because his grandmother would be going back to Hungary in the beginning of August, and we wanted her at the ceremony.

After Frank finished talking to them, his mother looked me right in the eye. I saw tears coming out of hers. I was a little scared because I didn't know if they were tears of happiness or not. But it took only a minute or less to find out. Right after our eyes met, she opened her arms wide, as if opening her heart.

"Come here, Nina," she said, "and give me a hug." She enveloped me in her arms.

"From now on, feel free to call us mom and dad," said Frank's father. I knew then that this was another sign from God. He was in control of everything.

We left the gym and went to his parents' house to celebrate the good news with Frank's sister and her husband. Together, we all decided that the ceremony should take place in their backyard. I called a marriage officiant and asked if she was available on July 24, at 5:00 p.m.

"Summer is always so busy and people usually book a year in advance," she said, "but you're very lucky. I normally leave an hour break between ceremonies for my commute. And since the weddings before and after yours are in the same neighbourhood, I can fit you in."

Thankfully, the marriage licence in British Columbia is issued at the time of application; we were at the local marriage licence issuer the following Monday. When we got there, we were so nervous, especially Frank, that the officer jokingly asked him, "Are you being forced to get married?"

Frank, indeed, seemed a little uncomfortable that day because I had offered to pay for the wedding expenses. Even though he agreed with my idea, after I insisted a lot, his pride was hurt. He wanted to be the one providing for all, but as a good wife-to-be, I couldn't let him spend any money on our wedding, not after I found out that he had a lot of other things to pay for.

A few days before we set the date and told our families, I asked Frank how he was doing with his finances. For a while, I had suspected that something was wrong because he never opened his bills. I had a lot of experience with that kind of behaviour, especially since I had worked in a bank for two years doing collections. When I was in debt, I had responded the same way to bills. Denial is a common practice among those who have financial troubles.

"Everything's under control," he said. "You shouldn't worry."

But I didn't believe him, mostly because the banks were calling every other day, looking for him. So, one day, I waited until he left for work. I opened all his mail. As I had imagined, Frank was in trouble. The amount he owed wasn't huge, but I was more disappointed by the fact that he didn't trust me enough to tell me the truth. Afraid that I was getting into another failed relationship, I cried.

Still crying, I began to pray, asking God for wisdom. I didn't know what to do. I knew that if we wanted a long and healthy marriage, we needed to add a lot of trust to our relationship. I grew up hearing people say, "It takes time to build trust," and that was what I believed. I wanted to marry Frank, but I wanted us to trust each other first. It seemed almost impossible for that to happen in such a short period of time. When he got home that night, I was too tired to start an argument. I thought the conversation would be much easier after a good night of rest.

The next morning, after breakfast, I invited Frank for a walk at the park. He was in a very good mood and made me laugh many times with his jokes. The whole time we were walking, I was praying in silence, asking, "God, please show me the right moment to start talking about his debt."

Only when we got back home did I have the courage to tell Frank I had opened the envelopes full of bills. He was so ashamed about the debt. More than anything, he thought that how he had gotten into that situation was too embarrassing to share. Many years before we had met, he was in a long-term relationship with a severally depressed girlfriend. He didn't know that she had to take medication to control her moods until the day he broke up with her.

Because of the depression, she was always fighting and crying over little things, blaming him at all times for her sadness. Frank never felt so miserable. Looking for an escape, and trying to avoid more conflict with her, he began to spend money without control. He was trying to fill the hole he felt in his Soul. Frank did realize that the way out wasn't the one he was going for; he wasted a lot of money and tried to fix the situation by borrowing more. But unfortunately, when that happened, it was already too late. The day I opened his bills, I found out that he had two credit cards maxed out, a mortgage refinanced, and a loan with a credit union.

Sorry for what he had done, Frank could barely look at me. I could see in his eyes how hurtful it was for him to admit that he needed help, so I told him about my own experiences. I tried to show him that he was not alone. We all make mistakes and if he had trusted in me before, it wouldn't have mattered to me.

That afternoon, he called me twice from work. In the first call, he apologized for keeping his debts secret from me and asked me not to give up on him. In the second call, he told me he prayed to the Lord, thanking Him for having me in his life.

Wait a minute, I thought. If Frank had truly prayed, it was because he had started to believe in God. This was a sign that everything could change because he had opened a door for God to enter into our relationship. That was the answer to my prayers. I knew God could do the impossible, for those who believe. Suddenly, I felt deep in my heart that it was really easy for me to love Frank. All that I could see in him was perfect. If I hadn't noticed anything irregular in his finances, I would never have had second thoughts about us. All of this had unfolded under God's plan.

I remembered the things I had done in my past. I was far from perfect. Yet, Jesus suffered for me on the cross, and I'm sure it wasn't easy for him. But as a result of that effort, I could then have a relationship with God that was filled with the most pure and genuine love. Thinking a little more about that, I came to the conclusion that true love is a result of the effort we make to love someone despite their imperfections. Just like Jesus loves us.

So, I called Frank back and assured him that I would not give up on us. I also told him that I had some money left over from the amount I brought with me. I offered to pay for the wedding expenses and to help him organize his financial situation so that we could pay off all of his debts.

Chapter 15

The Dream Dress and a One-dollar Diamond Ring

"For You, O Lord, will bless the righteous; With favor You will surround him as with a shield."

Psalm 5:12 (NKJV)

AS SOON AS FRANK made me aware of his whole financial situation, and allowed me to take control of the payments and expenses, I began to pray and ask God to help us. I asked for wisdom, for a promotion at Frank's job, and for my house in Brazil to be sold. I knew that God had helped me once, when I was in trouble, so I was sure that, somehow, He could blow the winds in our favour.

But I also knew, based on past experience, that we needed to do our part. So, Frank and I agreed that buying a diamond ring was out of the question. Of course, I would love to have had one; which woman would not?

But I knew that if I said that to Frank, he would probably use some extra credit to buy me one, and that would put us in more debt. Besides, it was never part of the tradition in Brazil to have the groom give a diamond ring to the bride. Instead, the couple usually wears matching wedding bands on their respective right hand, while engaged; at the wedding, they move the rings to their left hand.

We got a very nice pair of matching rings, for an affordable price. We asked to personalize them, engraving the phrase "only forever" inside each one. To make them look even more special, we wanted to add the letter "S" on his ring, and "F" on mine. But the jeweller where we bought the rings wasn't able to do the engraving for us. After checking in the Yellow Pages for personalized engraving, we found some stores in the mall close to our apartment. We rushed to the mall but none of the stores we found could do the kind of engraving we wanted. Frustrated, we decided to stop looking, to go home and try some place else another day. As we were heading to the parking lot, a banner from a famous jeweller caught our attention: it was advertising a diamond ring for only a dollar.

We looked at each other and started laughing. We both thought this was one of those "great deals" where taxes and fees cost more than a ring at its regular price.

But Frank was more curious than I was, so he grabbed my hand and pulled me towards the store. Already inside, he asked the young girl who approached us about the deal.

"Once a year, our company chooses a day where we offer a diamond ring for only a dollar to the first ten people who enter the store on that day."

It sounded too good to be true. I asked to see the rings. I wanted to check them out and see if there was something wrong with them. No, they were flawless. One was the prettiest. It was a modest yet elegant solitaire, in yellow gold, with a few sparkly little diamonds on the sides of a not-so-big diamond. Simple, but it felt classic and clean. Sophisticated. She let me try it on. It fit perfectly, as if it were custom made for me.

Frank saw the joy in my eyes while I was trying on the ring and asked for more details.

"When will you be selling those rings for a dollar?" he asked. "What time does the store open? Where do people line up, based on past years?" The store clerk gave us all the information we needed. We thanked her and left the store, still talking about how amazing the ring was, and how it fit me so well. It was a Wednesday afternoon. After the mall, Frank drove me home and went to work.

The rest of the week went by very fast. I was so busy with the wedding details I did not even notice that it was already Friday night. Frank started to pack some food, blankets, and an extra battery for his laptop.

"What's going on?" I asked him. "Are we going camping?"

Frank said nothing. It was almost 11:00 p.m.

"Where are we going?" I felt confused. "We are going to buy your diamond ring."

Anyone who knows Frank well knows that he loves adventures. But they also know that he is a really proud man. For him, sleeping overnight at a jeweller's door to buy a ring, even for a dollar, was something he would normally never do, but he did.

His ultimate goal was to make me happy. For that, he would spare no effort. So, he swallowed his pride, placed his sleeping bag on the floor outside the mall's main entrance door, covered his legs with a blanket, and played games on his phone. Without sleep, he watched movies and the World Cup match (Argentina vs Germany) from Friday night until 10 o'clock Saturday morning, when the mall's entrance doors finally opened. And I was there with him. I couldn't stay at home, in the comfort of my bed, knowing that my wonderful fiancé was alone, sitting on a hard sidewalk, on a cold night, for almost twelve hours, just so he could be the first one to enter the store and make sure no one else would pick the ring I loved.

When we entered the jewellery store, the same employee who spoke with us on Wednesday approached us, amazed by Frank's determination. We were the first ones to enter the store, just like Frank had said we would, and we got my ring, just as I had wanted. As we previously thought, taxes were not included in the advertised price. So, instead of only one dollar, my beautiful diamond ring cost us exactly one dollar and twelve cents. And the other rings we bought didn't go to waste; I wear both rings on the same finger and Frank wears his.

While we were planning the wedding, this was the first of a series of miracles. A friend from church, whom I call Tita B., felt very sad that nobody from my family would come to Canada for the ceremony. I understood why; there was not enough time for anybody from Brazil to apply for a visa, book vacation days, and buy tickets. To make things even more disappointing, every wedding dress I had liked, either to buy or rent, would cost us a lot of money and we didn't have much to spend.

Tita B. didn't know about our financial situation, but she had experience with weddings. She knew there are many hidden costs and unexpected expenses, even in a small ceremony like the one I was planning. She wanted to do something for me that would make me happy and help me lower costs. Since she used to work as a seamstress, making alterations and repairs, she offered to make my wedding dress. I could choose any dress, Tita B. told me, and she would make it the way I always dreamed. I was delighted.

I had lost count of how many times I had watched a movie called *27 Dresses*, which I really liked. The main character got married wearing a very simple dress—the most beautiful one I had ever seen. It was a white, taffeta, A-line gown with a V-shaped neckline and back. Under the waistline, raised just below the bust, the rest of the dress flowed to the floor. I looked on the Internet for a picture of the same dress and showed it to Tita B. She also loved the design. A few minutes later, she was already taking notes of my measurements. Then she took me with her to a store where we chose the fabric; that was the only thing she allowed me to pay for.

Just like she promised, Tita B. got the dress done the way I wanted. She also fixed Frank's suit. On the wedding day, she helped me get dressed and drove me in her white car to the venue (Frank's parents' house), just like a mother would do. For the ceremony, Frank's mother had decorated the entire living room with beautiful white-and-pink lilies, my favourite flowers.

On the morning of our wedding day, I went to a hair stylist and Frank went to pick up his best man at the airport. His longtime friend, Markos, came all the way from Saskatoon, Sask. just for that evening. Every little thing went well, extraordinarily uncomplicated. I did my own makeup, my mother-in-law decorated her house with some flowers, and we ordered food from our favourite Italian restaurant.

My family in Brazil could watch everything live through a webcam. After Frank and I had exchanged vows, the Brazilians opened a bottle of champagne at the same time we were opening ours in Canada. That way, we could all—Frank and I, our families, his best man, my maid of honour, my friend Alison, Tita B, and her husband— toast together. Then, those in Brazil turned off their computers and we went outside, to the backyard, where the party was held. We danced a lot and laughed a lot more. Frank never looked so handsome. I never felt so happy.

God's presence, a simple dress, a pair of rings, a small party, a few friends and our family: we didn't need a whole bunch of things to make that day the best of our lives.

After the party, we opened the wedding gifts and loved them all. We received practical ones such as home appliances, electronics, and some decorative items. Frank's parents, his sister, and grandmother also gave us a good amount of money that we could use to pay for the wedding meal and to start paying off some of our debts. (After the wedding, Frank and I had become one, so his debts became my debts as well.)

My mother also wanted to do something special, even more so because she was feeling truly sad for not being able to be present, in person, at the wedding. So, she decided to give us some money to spend on what we called our "honeymoon." A week after the wedding, Frank had a training camp in Ontario. From there, he was to fly to Singapore, with his athlete, to participate in the first edition of The Youth Olympic Games, where they would stay for twenty-one days. When I told my mom that Frank would be away for the entire month of August, she offered to pay for my ticket so that I could fly with him to Ontario.

She knew how important it would be, in our first month of marriage, if Frank and I could stay together at least for a week, even if only during the nights, after his work. Besides, August 5 is my birthday; if it wasn't for her gift, I would have had to spend that day alone in

Vancouver. Frank asked permission to take me with him to the camp, and the national coach saw no problem with this, as long as my presence wouldn't disturb Frank's training schedule.

My mother wanted to give us something we could always remember, and she did.

Chapter 16

Fasten Your Seat Belts: The Elephant is Taking Off

"But Jesus looked at them and said, 'With men it is impossible, but not with God; for with God all things are possible'."

Mark 10:27 (NKJV)

FRANK AND I WERE BOTH at the boarding area at Vancouver International Airport, waiting for our flight to Toronto. Since Frank was going on a business trip, the Canadian gymnastics team had booked and paid for his ticket. A few days after Frank had received his e-ticket, I had paid for mine with the money my mom gave us.

Thanks to God, I was able to find a place on the same flight as Frank, but because it was really full, I couldn't find any seat close to his. While we were checking in our luggage, I asked the young female agent, "Is there a cancellation by any chance? Did anybody upgrade from coach? This is sort of our honeymoon and we'd really like to sit together." "I'm sorry, but the flight is completely full," she said. "But maybe you'll have better luck if you talk to someone at the customer service counter." The middle-aged woman at this counter was beautiful and curvy with brown eyes and brown hair held back with a ribbon. But she sure wasn't very happy that day. She was very rude with us; we had barely opened our mouths when she said, "It's impossible for you to get seats together. The flight is fully booked."

"But it's our honeymoon," I pleaded. We thought that somehow, our story would melt her heart. "Well, then, you have a lifetime to be together," she replied, "so it shouldn't be a problem to sit apart today."

Even though we didn't appreciate the way she spoke to us, we were mostly dissatisfied with the outcome, so we asked to speak with the person in charge. When this nice man came out of his office, we learned that many parents were asking to sit with their children; keeping families with young kids seated together was a priority for the company.

"I can't promise you anything," he said, "but I'll take your recent marriage into consideration. You'll have to wait a bit for any decision. I hope that you can understand." A few minutes after we had talked to the supervisor, the guy working at the boarding gate started to call a lot of people by name. Most of them, parents and travellers with disabilities with their companions, all got their seats changed, as they had requested. Later, the same guy called a young couple that just happened to be sitting beside us.

"I'm sorry, but there are no seats left side by side," he told them. "You'll have to stick with your original booking." When Frank heard this, he looked at me and said, "Don't worry just yet. We can still trade with another passenger once we're on the plane."

Smiling, I looked into his eyes. "I'm not worried," I told him. "Ever since that scary lady told us it was impossible, I have been praying. I asked God to give us the seats, and I believe that He is able to keep us together always for as long as we live."

The whole time we were waiting, Frank was busy playing with his phone, and I was talking to Jesus. I was reminding Him that after that trip to Toronto with Frank, I would be alone for twenty-one days, and that during our "honeymoon" I would only see Frank in the evenings. I finished my prayer by thanking Him. Compared to the need of many people around the world, what I was asking for was a luxury, just a plus; but I felt comfortable asking Him regardless because I knew there was nothing impossible for Him. Like the Bible says: *For with God nothing will be impossible"* (Luke 1:37 (NKJV).

When my dearest but skeptical husband heard that, he shook his head and said, "God is probably busy with more important things. We should stick to my plan of trying to trade seats."

In less than a minute, we were called at the gate. When we got there, the same guy who had said no to the other couple spoke to us.

"Congratulations on your wedding," he said. "I wish you both happiness. Here are your new seat numbers." I looked at Frank and smiled. He seemed dumbfounded.

As we were entering the plane, I held Frank's hands and whispered into his ear: "Can you see now? There is nothing impossible for God." And we travelled, together, side by side, just like in love and marriage.

A few hours later, we arrived in Toronto, where we rented a car and drove fifty-seven kilometres southwest to the Burlington, Ont., where the training camp would be held. Our hotel was in downtown Burlington, beside Spencer Smith Park, on the shores of Lake Ontario, where I spent most of my afternoons enjoying the sun and water. The park was beautiful, had a small beach, many walking paths and a Centennial Pond, where kids were playing with model sailboats. Every day, Frank would leave early in the morning for work and come back around 6:00 p.m. Once, or twice, he was able to come back at noon, to have lunch with me, but most of the time, I was completely alone during the day. For the first two days, I stayed in my room, watching movies and reading books in the morning. In the afternoon, I went down to the park. I was trying to stay safe since I didn't know the place or anybody in Ontario.

But on the third day, alone in the hotel, I began to replay in my mind memories from when I had the chance to travel to other states in Brazil. Fearless, I used to organize my own sightseeing excursions. This made me realize that, once again, I was letting fear take control of me. I was wasting the amazing opportunity that God had given me, through my mother's wedding gift, to explore and learn about new places. So, I decided to shake off all my fears and trust that God would keep me protected. I went for my first walk away from the hotel and park.

On the fourth day, I was feeling a lot more confident, so I stretched my faith a little farther. I rented a bicycle, took a map, and planned a trip to the Royal Botanical Gardens, the largest of its kind in Canada, on the border of Burlington and Hamilton, Ont. Frank and I had lunch together, and as soon as he left to work, I went on my adventure. I promised him that I would be back before 6:00 p.m., since we had made plans to have dinner at a nice local restaurant to celebrate our honeymoon.

According to the map, it would take me about a half-hour to get there. But after thirty minutes on my bike, I was still not even close to the Gardens. Already used to seeing my plans not go exactly as intended, it was no surprise to me to realize that I had gone in the wrong direction. Somewhere along my way, I had missed an exit and gotten lost.

Without any sign of a network available on my cell phone, I didn't know what to do or how to look for help. (Terrible at following maps, I can easily get lost, even when driving in a familiar area and using a GPS system. I'm better at following God's instructions.) I was about to start panicking when I stopped in front of a huge factory and began to pray to God, asking Him to help me find my way. A few minutes later, I felt peace in my heart. I decided it was best to turn around and follow the same route I had taken back to Spencer Smith Park. Only then should I start my trip, again, to the Gardens. So, I went back to the park and one hour later, arrived, exhausted, at the Royal Botanical Gardens.

I've been privileged to see amazing places that men and God have built together, but this place was far beyond astounding. I only stayed for two hours, but could certainly have spent an entire day walking, watching birds, smelling flowers, taking pictures, and listening to the band playing jazz. I felt a sense of peace and happiness that made me think about eternity in heaven.

Later, Frank and I went out for our honeymoon dinner. At the restaurant, he told me: "Tomorrow, I'll have the afternoon off, so we can do whatever you want."

It was August 5, my birthday. "Let's celebrate at the African Lion Safari."

The next day, Frank and I had such a great time at this Hamilton, Ont. tourist attraction. We watched the elephants swimming and I fed animals at the pets' corner. Frank had a great conversation with one of the parrots. We laughed, watching the monkeys climb onto cars and steal food from people. We took a ride on the safari tour bus and on a boat called *African Queen*, which didn't look like the one in the movie. We saw many animals, from antelopes, camels, deer, giraffes, lions, zebras, and rhinoceros to monkeys and bats and all sorts of birds such as vultures, toucans, pigeons, owls, hawks, cranes, and cockatoos. I felt completely satisfied, but God had something extra reserved for me, something above and beyond what I had asked for: an elephant ride! At first, Frank thought it was too silly and refused to go. But a nice woman standing beside us reminded him: "Hey, it's an opportunity that only happens once in a lifetime. It would be crazy to miss it." I still thank God for putting that woman in our lives. She not only persuaded Frank to go for the ride, but also offered to take pictures of us as we were up on the elephant's back. We both rode on the same one with me in front and Frank behind, holding my waist. We petted it gently, touching its thick skin and hair, which felt more like steel wire, while the largest of all land animals moved quietly and carefully.

We left African Lion Safari only when they closed their gates. It was the best birthday I ever had.

Frank's training camp finished on Friday that same week; his flight to Singapore was booked for the following Monday. That gave us the weekend to enjoy being together before he left on another long trip. On Saturday, we spent most of the day at the quaint, theatre town of Niagara-on-the-Lake, Ont. We went for a tour around the village in a horse-drawn carriage and had lunch at an historic restaurant.

After lunch, we drove to Niagara Falls, about twenty kilometres away, where we got onto *The Maid of the Mist*, a white, double-decker catamaran that fits 600 passengers. It took us very close to the waterfalls. We were so close that we could barely hear each other over the powerful roar of the waves. The spray from the falls and resulting mist nearly kept my eyes closed and we had to wear a long rain poncho to prevent our clothes from getting completely soaked. We stayed at the falls until night time, so we could see them lit up, reflecting every colour of the rainbow beautifully.

On Monday morning, at Toronto airport, my sweet husband walked me to my gate and kissed me goodbye. It was truly sad seeing him go away, knowing that we would be apart for so long. But at the same time, I was happy because as my mother had wished, we had an amazing adventure together in Ontario—something we will always remember.

I arrived in Vancouver about five hours later. Frank and his young athlete arrived on the other side of the world thirty-two hours after that.

Chapter 17

Waiting in the Wings

"But let patience have its perfect work, that you may be perfect and complete, lacking nothing."

James 1:4 (NKJV)

AS SOON AS FRANK RETURNED from Singapore, we mailed out, all at once, the documents and forms for Frank's sponsorship for my permanent residency, my work visa, and permanent residency application. We had read on the Canadian Immigration website that the process could take one to two years to be completed. Because I was applying from inside the country, I was allowed to remain in Canada until an answer was made, but I couldn't work, study or leave the country while waiting.

We also read that nothing we could do would help to speed things up. Well, I firmly believe they were not considering the power of a prayer when they added that footnote. These words from the Bible came to me: *"Ask of Me, and I will give You the nations for Your inheritance, and the ends of the earth for Your possession"* (Psalm 2:8 (NKJV)).

Looking on the Internet for a local Pentecostal church, I found one close to my home that made me feel welcomed and loved. The church held weekly sermons on Sundays, and on Wednesday mornings, a group of eight or ten women used to meet so we could worship the Lord and pray together for each other's needs. At one time, we were all praying for me, asking God to have my process approved since I wanted to be sure that I could stay in Canada, with Frank, for good. Besides, I also wanted to start working as soon as possible and help him fix our financial situation.

While we were still praying for me and my needs, one of the women said in a loud voice: "Place her papers on top of the pile, Lord." Sure enough, nine months later, we had Frank's sponsorship approved along with my permanent resident status.

I called my mother-in-law to share the good news, "But it's way too soon to hear back from the immigration people," she told me. "I know from past experience." Thinking I was mistaken, she only believed it was true when I took my confirmation of permanent residence to her house. Nobody from Frank's family or any of our friends who immigrated to Canada had ever had their process approved in such a short time frame.

Looking back now, I see that it all happened really fast. It was definitely a miracle. But while I was waiting, it certainly didn't seem like that. A silent wait, it was one of the most difficult times I ever went through. We didn't see any progress, didn't know what was going on, or what the outcome would be. The only thing we could control was our emotions, and that wasn't an easy task. We were forced to learn how to let go and not worry about things that weren't in our hands, to trust more in God, and to believe that He always has our best interest in mind.

So we prayed and waited, impatiently, many times I had so many nightmares that tormented me a lot. In all of them, Frank and I were apart and couldn't see each other. I was always trying to reach him on the phone but he never answered. After Singapore, Frank travelled to India and Hungary that same year, in 2010. We had horrible arguments over the phone because I was so insecure, afraid that those dreams meant something. I almost destroyed my marriage even before our first anniversary. But thankfully, God was in control. He never lets his children be snatched away from His hands and blessings. As the Bible says: *"And I give them eternal life, and they shall never perish; neither shall anyone snatch them out of My hand"*

John 10:28 (NKJV). So, one Sunday at church, He prompted me to approach the pastor after the sermon and tell him about my nightmares.

I was so embarrassed to say that I was almost thirty and still had a fear of nightmares, but I did. I stood in front of him, gave him a firm handshake, and asked for help. The pastor told me: "The Lord uses dreams to communicate with us and so does Satan. See, he uses nightmares to stir fear in our souls. His strategy is to fill our hearts with doubt. When we doubt, we sin, and sin moves us away from God."

I let the pastor's words sink in. I decided that instead of letting those night terrors transform my waiting time into misery, I would use my spare time to have fun and accomplish old dreams, like writing the first words of this book, for example. Without a trace, those nightmares disappeared. Today, I have no record of the last time I even had one.

As I took the first step, the Lord took care of the rest.

I switched the negative images of my bad dreams into positive memories of things I never thought I would experience like sticking my tongue out to taste the cold, soft touch of a snowflake falling from the sky, on the day I saw snow for the first time. Or like the smell of wood burning while Frank was teaching me how to roast marshmallows outside our tent, at our favourite campground, by the Cultus Lake, located on the south side of Chilliwack, a city just about one hour east of Vancouver, BC. Or like the time in the zoo, when this huge bald eagle sitting on my arm stretched its wings behind my back as if it was hugging me.

Life is filled with beautiful events like these. Sadly, we often forget to appreciate them because of our busy routines or because we are so hooked on bad experiences, we don't make room for new and better ones.

The following year, in 2011, I had the opportunity to show my mother the benefits of stretching our wings, embracing new adventures, and accumulating good memories. Since I couldn't leave the country until my immigration process was done, and didn't know how long it would take until I could go back to Brazil to see my family, I suggested that my mom and brother should come to Canada for a visit. Even though she was very excited, my mother's bad experiences had taught her that a safe place to be was a place without dreams, where she couldn't be disappointed. So, after she applied for her visitor's visa, she wasn't confident that it would be approved.

While we were waiting for an answer from the consulate, I was always happy, trying to pass that same confidence onto her, either by showing how I was preparing the apartment to accommodate them or sharing the itinerary that I had planned for us. My mother, on the other hand, had not even prepared her luggage. As I was expecting, she and my brother got their visas approved. I knew that God is able to do far more than we can ask or think. A few days later, they arrived in Vancouver in March. As soon as we got home, I quoted a verse from the Bible to my mother: *"Now to Him who is able to do exceedingly abundantly above all that we ask or think, according to the power that works in us"* Ephesians 3:20 (NKJV). This was something I wrote down a long time ago while still living in Brazil. I never imagined that one day, I would be hosting my mom and brother at my husband's apartment in Canada. And my mom understood that. The entire time she was in Canada, she repeated that verse over and over: every time we had a great time together, when we visited places she thought she would never be able to see, when she and Marcelo met Frank's family and got along very well, and when they were blessed with snow in spring time.

God wanted to heal her lack of trust and belief, showing that by His grace, every dream becomes real. If we truly believe He is who He says He is, and that He loves us, we should live our lives expecting to receive nothing but good things from Him. Like the Bible says: *"Or what man is there among you who, if his son asks for bread, will give him a stone? Or if he asks for a fish, will he give him a serpent? If you then, being evil, know how to give good gifts to your children, how much more will your Father who is in heaven give good things to those who ask Him!"* (Matthew 7:9-11 (NKJV)).

While my mom was in Canada, she told me that someone had shown interest in buying the house I was building in Brazil. But she didn't have more details about the offer because the owner of the other half (Tom) was making things difficult for the sale. They had even gotten into an argument a few days before she came to visit me. I knew that only by a miracle, and with God's approval, could the house be sold for a fair price, but I also knew what He was able to do. So, I got really excited and began to praise the Lord for that possibility. I started to pray for peace between all who were involved in that transaction, including me.

Thankfully, Frank and I didn't have to wait until the house was sold to start paying off some of our debts. As we took action and stopped dining out and buying things we didn't need, we were able to raise some money to pay off and cancel some of his credit cards. To keep us from falling into temptation, Frank agreed to cut up the ones we couldn't pay off.

Suddenly, money that we had not even expected started to arrive. We would open our mail box and a cheque would be there waiting for us. Or a person would ask Frank for private gymnastics lessons and pay him a good amount of money.

I praised God at all times, thanking him for what He was doing in our lives, and tried to make sure that Frank was always close by, listening.

Chapter 18

Mi Casa, Su Casa, Jesus

"And if it seems evil to you to serve the Lord, choose for yourselves this day whom you will serve, whether the gods which your fathers served that were on the other side of the River, or the gods of the Amorites, in whose land you dwell. But as for me and my house, we will serve the Lord."

Joshua 24:15 (NKJV)

WHEN I WAS TWENTY, I found out that I had endometriosis.

I was watching a movie at the cinema in Brazil when I felt a huge pain in my back. It was so strong that I passed out. At the hospital, I was told that I had endometrial tissue deposited in my left ovary. As the endometrium got thicker, broke down, and bled every month as part of my menstrual period, so did that little tissue. But because there wasn't a way for that blood to exit the ovary, it resulted in inflammation. The doctors told me that a pregnancy would be the natural way to treat and control my condition. But I decided to try medications instead since I knew that I didn't want to be with Tom much longer.

During my treatment, I offered God a sacrifice for my healing: I promised I would go to five different churches and light a candle on their respective altars if He could, indeed, heal me. Because I didn't know Jesus in my heart then, I didn't know that this wasn't necessary; He had already done that for me, on the cross. But God was gracious enough to understand my ignorance. After a laparoscopy surgery, which inserts a fibre-optic instrument through the abdominal wall, and a cycle of three months of heavy medications, the doctors found no residue of that tissue in my ovary or elsewhere in my abdomen.

God did me a favour. I was healed. In return, I kept my word and fulfilled my part of the deal. I went to five churches and lit the five candles.

Now back (I mean, ahead) to 2011, when I was thirty. A few months after my mom and brother had left Canada and gone back to Brazil, I was at church on Mother's Day. The sermon was about God's healing power. Immediately, I remembered what He had done for me when I was sick and in pain. An overwhelming feeling entered my heart, and I began to cry. I had finally understood the work of Jesus on the cross. On that same day, I felt God prompting me to stop taking birth control pills and start trying to conceive.

When I got home from church, I talked to Frank.

"I think we should start trying to have a baby," I said. We had no idea what the answer for my permanent resident application would be and we still hadn't paid off what we were owing. As crazy as it sounds, Frank said, "Yes!" Right away, we threw the medication that we had left into the garbage.

Driven by the thought of me getting pregnant and because my house in Brazil was almost sold, Frank and I decided to look for a bigger place than the apartment we were living in. We knew that to get a new mortgage approved, we would need to fix Frank's credit report. As soon as possible, I had to start working to build my credit history in Canada. But these realities didn't affect us negatively; they only motivated us even more. We were determined to do as much as we could to save money for a down payment.

We spent most of our time dreaming and looking for apartments. We found some beautiful ones, and they were all a lot better than the apartment we had. But for some reason, none of them seemed to fit our needs.

Although we were so excited about the idea of moving to a new place and starting fresh, we never felt peace or joy visiting these places. Once, we thought we had found a suitable townhouse but ended up cancelling the contract within the cooling-off period because a few hours later, I was too frightened that we had picked a place impulsively, without thinking or praying beforehand.

After that episode, we came to the conclusion that we needed to take a break and wait until I could start working before going back to house-hunting. That summer, on July 27, 2011, I became a permanent resident of Canada. Hurray! No more waiting and worry and wondering if I would be allowed to stay in my newly adopted country. One week earlier, Frank and I were camping when we received a call from Hungary, informing us that one of his uncles, someone he really loved, had passed away from lung cancer. That was a truly sad moment, yet thankfully, it prompted the end of Frank's smoking habit. What blessings were flowing into my life.

For an entire year, I had prayed and asked God to help Frank quit smoking cigarettes. I couldn't stand the smell and knew that they weren't good for his health either. At first, I didn't know what to do to help him quit, so we fought a lot. But then I realized that only God has the power to fix us; we are not able to fix ourselves, much less others, so I decided to let it go. I began to pray and allowed God to do His work, in his time.

I don't believe that Frank's uncle needed to die so he could stop smoking, but the Bible says that all things work together for good to those who love God: *"And we know that all things work together for good to those who love God, to those who are then called according to His purpose"* (Romans 8:28 (NKJV)). I firmly believe that all things means all good *and* bad things as well. And many other good things happened to us after that very sad moment.

Usually, when immigrants like me become a permanent resident, they receive a card that proves their status in Canada. When they return to Canada from a trip to another country, it allows them to enter and stay in Canada. Called the "PR Card," this document is usually delivered by mail, twenty-three days after the recipient signs a record of landing. Only after that can immigrants apply for a social insurance number, which allows them to work anywhere in Canada.

There was nothing that Frank and I could do but wait a little more until I could finally apply for a job. We both agreed that the best way to wait was to enjoy the last bit of summer and go camping again. This time, we headed for a campground near Kelowna in British

Columbia's interior. On our way there, we drove by a brand new complex of apartments and townhouses, in Langley, BC that caught our attention. We decided to park our car and take a good look at the options in the show suites at the presentation centre.

We absolutely loved one specific floor plan and all the features: the finishing, location, as well as the payment conditions. But because we had a history of being impulsive and getting into trouble, we decided we should go on our road trip. We would use that time to study the pros and cons and pray about it, asking God to give us peace in our hearts if that was something He had prepared for us.

I called my mother and told her about this amazing place we were praying for.

"We both loved everything in it, and really hope we can buy it," I said. "Do you have any news about the sale of my house in Brazil?"

"Believe it or not, all the people involved in the deal just came to an agreement recently. It looks like it will only take you about fifteen days to finish the sale and receive the money. What timing you have!"

A week after that, Frank and I drove back to Langley and stopped again at the presentation centre. We left our emotions in the car and went through all the show suites again. This time, we paid particular attention to details such as granite countertops, hardwood floors, stainless-steel appliances, and things that add value in case of resale. We realized that for a little more money, we could afford a townhouse in that same complex, with all the features we loved, plus a nice, quiet backyard—a big one for a townhouse.

According to the realtor, we had five days to hold the place and think more about the huge step we were going to take. Even though we were sure it was exactly what we wanted, we needed more than five days to close the sale in Brazil and transfer the money to Canada. Frank and I asked to speak with the developer, and the realtor gave us his phone number. We went home and I had time for a quick prayer before Frank called him. The developer agreed to give us the time we needed. Thanks to God, the money for the initial down payment arrived from Brazil two days before we expected it.

We signed the purchase and sale agreement to our new townhouse in the first week of September. Because I had not yet received my PR card, I had to show my passport as proof of identification. The PR card arrived two weeks later.

As soon as I opened the mail and saw the PR card, I was able to apply for my social insurance number. We ran to the closest Service Canada centre and they provided the number right away. Things were going amazingly well with us; to make them even better, I just needed to start working. I sent out some résumés and prayed to God to open the doors of a good and fair employer.

Since I had given my résumé to a headhunter, it didn't take much of a wait until my phone rang with a job proposal. The same cable company we had chosen to provide us service was hiring young people to start a new department of outbound sales. Even though it was an entry-level position, they were offering full-time work and all benefits from day one. Later, we learned that this was a huge privilege (I called it a miracle) since everybody else in the company, except the HR team and executives, had to start as a part-time employee; only after some months could they apply for a full-time position.

I didn't care about the wage, or how much commission I could make. I did not even know that Frank and I were eligible for the company's benefits until the first day of training. I just said, "Yes, I want the job." The only thing I really wanted was to have our mortgage approved. I was positive that Our Heavenly Father had His hands all over it. He knew exactly what we needed, and that was His answer to my prayer.

And God didn't stop there. Touched by the series of miracles he had witnessed since I moved to Canada, Frank decided to take the first step towards a beautiful relationship with the Lord. After almost two years of prayers, I finally had my husband attending Sunday sermons with me. A few weeks later, while we were watching a sermon online in our living room, Frank stood up from the couch and prayed the salvation prayer. He said: "Jesus, I present myself to You. I pray and ask you to be Lord over my life. Forgive my sins, Jesus. Come into my heart. I believe this moment that I am saved. Amen." This is how he Frank prayed the salvation prayer and gave his life to Jesus.

Then we enjoyed an amazing wedding gift from my parents-in-law: a free trip to Mexico at an all-inclusive resort. It was my first international trip since I had left Brazil. What a way to finish the year and celebrate the beginning of a season of good breaks.

Chapter 19

Sales? No Sweat!

"And God is able to make all grace abound toward you, that you, always having all sufficiency in all things, may have an abundance for every good work."

2 Corinthians 9:8 (NKJV)

I MADE OUTBOUND SALES for the cable company for one year. I would call the customers who had chosen our competitors to offer similar services, usually for a better price. The phone conversations could range from very relaxed, funny, and enjoyable to extremely rude, insulting, and abusive. Some customers would ask to have a service added or ask for advice, but mostly, we heard people complaining about something either we did wrong, or they did. But no matter whose fault it was, we were always the target of their inflamed darts of rage. Nobody at work or at home likes to answer a company's 1-800-number calls, especially when the person on the other end of the line has an accent. Since English isn't my first language, I had to go through some rough times, dealing with racist comments. Even in a country like Canada, where multiculturalism is reflected in law, we still had to deal with some very racist people on a daily basis. After a couple of calls, I had to run to the washroom to cry, but I never thought about quitting, like many of my colleagues did. Since I was determined to get our mortgage approved, I was willing to do whatever it took, even if that meant I cried every day after every conversation.

The work environment in a call centre is a lot different than what many of us might think. Previously, as a costumer, I always thought that people were playing on their cell phones or taking coffee breaks while I was holding on the other end of the line, listening to some horrible song. But that is not the reality; there is a lot of pressure to make sales and there are many calls to answer. In the company's view, people are numbers. Everything is measured. Time is money. We had to keep track of the company's numbers, the amount of calls we answered, how many minutes we spent between calls, how we fixed the customer issues or how many washroom breaks we took.

The Bible says that those who are humbled will be exalted. Day after day, I kept repeating that in my mind. In the Bible's words: *"And whoever exalts himself will be humbled, and he who humbles himself will be exalted"* (Matthew 23:12 (NKJV)).

I would often visualize Frank and me having a cup of coffee in our backyard, enjoying the sunset; that was the reward I was looking for, for my endurance and resilience.

But God had planned something extra. Thanks to Him, who makes all things possible, after one month struggling with new words and angry costumers, I was able to improve my poor vocabulary. Soon I became one of the top performers in the department and made a lot of money. The sales began to happen naturally. I didn't need to push products that people didn't need or tell half-truth stories about our competitors to get their attention. The very thing I used to engage a conversation with them was my accent. The customers loved to hear my stories about Brazil, soccer, our food, and culture. I often suggested places in Brazil to visit. And that is my big secret about having success in sales: Make friends. People are more inclined to buy things when they are recommended by a friend.

With both of us working full-time, it didn't take long for Frank and I to pay off the last credit card bill and start putting money aside for our new house. At the bank, we were told that I needed to apply for a credit card to build a credit history in Canada, but I was seriously resistant to do so after all we had gone through. Yet, since our car was really old and the monthly costs of keeping it running were similar to payments on a new one, we decided to sell it and get a new car in my name. That way, we could solve two problems at once.

We posted an ad with photos of our car on a well-known website of classified advertising. For a whole week nobody showed any interest and we were contemplating lowering the price when our phone rang. Someone asked to see the car. We agreed to meet him the following morning, but he never showed up. (I still thank God for that person who stood us up. Because of him, we realized that our car needed a jump; the battery had run out when we tried to warm it up in preparation for the meeting. We certainly would have embarrassed ourselves trying to show that our car was working fine.)

That same day, a young couple called me, asking if they could see the car. When they arrived, I gave them the keys and let them drive the vehicle around. They loved it and paid for it right there. If wasn't for that first guy who didn't show up, we wouldn't have sold the car that day. Even if he had been interested in it, he would likely have tried to lowball the price and we probably would have lost money. Instead, we were paid the same amount we had asked for and used it towards the down payment for our new house.

After Frank and I got rid of our unnecessary debts, we put all the money we made into our savings account. We kept our strategy of not eating out and not buying things unless we really needed them. At all times, even during the tough ones, when we had to pay a lot of bills and didn't have any idea where to start, we were faithful with our tithes.

I understand how hard it is to give away money when you need it. I struggled a lot to give the tithe upon selling the house in Brazil because ten percent of that amount was a lot bigger than what I used to tithe every month, from my salary. That same amount could have paid one of our credit cards bills in full. I wrestled with my thoughts for about a week, wondering if I should pay the bill first and tithe later. But then I realized that the origin of my struggle was in my lack of faith. If I really trusted that God would provide for all my necessities and give me enough to supply for the needs of others, I would have given that money as soon as it was deposited in my account and wouldn't have kept it for a week, as I did.

We all face situations in which our faith is tested. It doesn't matter in what or whom you believe; there will always come a time when you will have to take a stand and prove that you are absolutely confident in putting your hope in something or someone. The difference between the person I used to be and who I want to be relies on who I decided to trust. When I took a leap of faith and obeyed God, giving the money I needed back to him, I did so because I reminded myself of what He had done for me in the past, and that He would never let me down. I wish I had never doubted that He would provide all my needs and had, instead, given the money right away. But a beautiful thing about being a child of God is to know that we are a work-in-progress. There will always be another opportunity to do what's right and stand up for what we believe.

And sure enough, my opportunity arrived a few months later.

On the contract for the purchase of our new home, August 22 was the closing date. Since the spring, we had put our old apartment on the market but no one had come to take a look at it. We changed the asking price three times. We added a lot of features, such as a free home-theatre system and furniture, trying to make it more attractive. But still, no one showed up. Since we were running out of time, our realtor called Frank and suggested that we should sell our new home. She knew we couldn't afford to pay two mortgages and the strata rules for the apartment didn't allow us to rent it. Besides that, we were counting on the money from the sale of our old place to complete the amount missing in the down payment for the townhouse.

Since Frank was busy working and couldn't give the realtor much attention, he asked her to call me instead. He told her: "I'll agree with whatever you and my wife decide is best to do."

The realtor called me and spent almost a half-hour lecturing me about bad decisions. She gave me a hard time for buying a new place before we had listed our existing apartment and finished her speech by saying, "You should start praying to at least get something back from the townhouse sale."

Quietly, I listened to all she had to say, not because I agreed with her, but mostly out of respect. But as soon as she finished, I told her with a calm, firm voice, "If you truly believe in the power of a prayer, as you suggested to me, then you should also believe that our apartment will sell on time." And I ended our conversation with these words: "Under no circumstances are you allowed to even think about selling our new house."

"As you wish," she replied.

After she hung up, I started to praise God out loud in the middle of the street. People might have thought I was crazy, but I didn't care. Thanks to God, who filled me with the presence of the Holy Spirit, I could perceive the enemy trying to steal my dream from me. It didn't matter how much the realtor tried to pressure me to quit—I knew that God was with me. So, I stood up for what I believed, and I truly believed that this new house was a gift from Him.

Years earlier, when I woke up that night, back in Brazil, with the feeling that He was calling me, He promised me that one day, I would have a house, a family, a new life. And The Lord I serve never breaks a promise. To embarrass the enemy, He sent a young couple to visit the apartment a day after our conversation with the realtor. The couple, the only two people who ever went to check out the place, made an offer. That same day, we accepted it.

The buyers agreed to move into the apartment on August 23, which was perfect because, according to our plans, we would have the keys to our new home on August 22. But one week before our moving day, the builder informed us that they were a little behind. They needed to change the closing date to September 22.

Aargh. My parents-in-law suggested that we stay with them, instead of at a hotel, so we could use the money saved to decorate the new house.

The big day (September 22) arrived. Our lawyer informed us that some paperwork between the city and the developer wasn't ready, but the developer was willing to keep their part of the deal and let us move into the new home in an escrow condition. This meant that we could live in our new place as tenants and would only start paying for the mortgage when the title was transferred into our name.

So, that's what we did. All together, we enjoyed four months of huge savings. That allowed us, in only one year, to buy new furniture and travel to Hungary, Mexico, and Brazil. That was my first time in Europe and our first time together in Brazil since Frank and I had met.

Chapter 20

Baptized in Clean, Cold Waters

"Now as they went down the road, they came to some water. And the eunuch said, 'See, here is water. What hinders me from being baptized?' Then Philip said, 'If you believe with all your heart, you may.' And he answered and said, 'I believe that Jesus Christ is the Son of God.'"

Acts 8:36-37 (NKJV)

MANY PEOPLE MIGHT THINK that the life of a believer is always easy and without troubles. But it seems to me that sometimes, we face more difficulties than others who aren't believers.

Not long after Frank gave his life to the Lord, he had to face one of the hardest situations in his professional life. The gym in Richmond, BC where he works was going through some changes. Some members of the board of directors weren't acting fairly with him and his family and were running the financial operations so poorly that the gym would soon have to close its doors. Frank had to step up and battle against these people, hiring lawyers and gathering witnesses to testify on his and his family's behalf. Thankfully, he won the battle and the incompetent directors left the board of the club.

But as a result, Frank lost some of his most talented athletes. The disgruntled directors who had left the gym started to call other parents. They tried to convince them that the gym would not survive without their hands-on administrative skills. They were so determined to make Frank pay back for what happened to them they even tried starting a rumour, saying that he wasn't good with the kids, that he used to treat them badly.

From the outside, it looked like Frank's career was being destroyed. There was nothing we could do but pray and wait for God's justice. Seeing my loving husband going through such an unfair situation really broke my heart. We prayed a lot. I kept speaking words of encouragement and reminding him that Jesus suffered a greater injustice for loving us.

I also shared with him a similar experience I went through while still working at the bank in Brazil, after I had led our team to join a company-wide strike. As soon as we got back to our activities, the branch manager called me and my colleagues to a roundtable session. One by one, my co-workers were forced to say why they thought I wasn't a good fit for the company. Therefore, I should resign.

"If I hadn't paid attention to the verse I read that morning in the Bible, I'm sure I would have probably yelled and screamed and been suspended," I told Frank. The verse said: *"But when they arrest you and deliver you up, do not worry beforehand, or premeditate what you will speak. But whatever is given you in that hour, speak that; for it is not you who speak, but the Holy Spirit"* (Mark 13:11 (NKJV)). As I told Frank, I kept myself quiet through the entire meeting at the bank, listening to people who used to be friends say things that I doubt they really thought or believed. When the manager forced me to say something in my defense, I just said: "Thank you for the feedback. I will take everything you said into consideration." Not having anything else to do or say, and frustrated because he didn't get me to lose my self-control, the manager dismissed us. That same day, I spent my entire commute thanking God for His guidance and protection.

Based on this experience and everything God had done for us in the last few years, Frank and I decided we would trust His ways and keep a good attitude towards everybody, including those who were opposing Frank. We also decided not to talk about either the situation or the revenge-filled people to anyone. If people insisted on knowing what had happened, we would use only kind words, trying to respect our enemies, even though we knew they didn't deserve it.

During this rough time for Frank, I was promoted to a senior position at work and received a huge salary raise. What truly amazed Frank and me was that I had applied to eleven junior opportunities within the company; none was considered a perfect fit. That made us think how silly I was for getting upset, trying so hard to fit into a junior position when God's plan was a lot better than mine. We learned a lesson from this. We decided that we would not worry about explaining ourselves or try to convince people that Frank and his family were the victims and not the bad guys in the gym management story. We would not bother trying to make those who did us wrong pay for what they had done. We simply let it go and let God do things according to His will.

That took a lot of pressure off our shoulders. With time, things started to get better for Frank in the club. With the remaining athletes working harder and Frank sharing his faith with them, the atmosphere at the gym suddenly became filled with joy. Results couldn't have been greater. Frank's athletes won the gold and silver medals in each category of every competition in which they competed in the province. And his oldest athlete, at age twenty-one, was nominated as national team member to represent New Zealand at the 2015 Summer Universiade (FISU) in Gwangju, South Korea and at the 2015 World Gymnastics Championships in Glasgow, Scotland, UK (he had dual citizenship). These victories reflected the presence of the Lord, and Frank and his athletes' talent for gymnastics. What was meant to harm Frank, to make him a resentful and bitter person, turned out to be a breakthrough in his career and in his personal relationship with God.

Around that time, my mother-in-law met a Brazilian family that had moved to her neighbourhood in Surrey, BC. They were missionaries who had left their entire life back in Brazil—family, friends, and a career as successful dentists—to follow their calling to love and serve people in Canada. Through them we met three other couples, all Brazilians, all Christians. It didn't take much for our friendship to grow stronger, and I couldn't thank God enough for them. Since I moved to Canada, I had begun to pray, asking for friends who shared the same values and faith. They were the answer to my prayers. We joined them in a Bible study group during the winter, where we had the opportunity to learn a lot about living in community and how God shapes people in different ways. When summer arrived, we took some time off from Bible study but we were so attached to each other that we kept hanging out together, which was great.

That same summer, in 2013, my mother and sister came to Canada to visit us. They loved our new home and our new Brazilian friends. Together, we all witnessed a missionary friend from Brazil baptize Frank, alone, in the waters of Alouette River, a tributary of the Pitt River in southwestern B.C. (Later, we learned that "alouette" is a French word for a lark, a bird known for singing while flying and announcing the coming of the day). Just like in olden times, as Jesus's disciple John used to baptize people in the Jordan River, Frank decided he wanted to be baptized in Alouette River. He chose this river because we loved the area and spent most of our summers going to Alouette Lake; the water is clean and incredibly blue. It was a warm and beautiful day, but according to Frank, who was immersed in the waters, it was freezing.

I admit that since the day Frank prayed the Salvation Prayer, I had spent many nights laying my hands over his body while he was sleeping, asking the Holy Spirit to touch his heart and stir in him the desire to be baptized in waters and in the Spirit as a public confirmation of his faith in Jesus.

But I confess that even in my most perfect dream, I never imagined witnessing such an event and feeling the mix of joy and relief when I saw Frank emerging from the river, saved, and free from a past that Jesus had just washed white and clean. It was such a confirmation that He had taken this important step in his faith.

Chapter 21

Bitter and Twisted

"The heart knows its own bitterness, And a stranger does not share its joy."

Proverbs 14:10 (NKJV)

THESE CRYPTIC JOURNAL notations provided no inkling of the anguish I was experiencing in November 2012:

Days late: 3

2 home pregnancy tests: negative

Beta HCG [the pregnancy hormone] < 1

This last reading meant I wasn't pregnant. If a woman is pregnant, the Beta HCG should range between 5 and 50mIU/ml, three weeks from the last menstrual period. Mine showed below 1mIU/ml. (This pharmacological measurement of weight to volume refers to milli-international units (1,1,000 g) per millilitre. It reveals how much hormone is in a urine or blood sample.)

As I already mentioned, I stopped taking birth control pills on Mother's Day 2011, after praying at church during a sermon about healing, even though I knew I was already healed from endometriosis. I was afraid that this condition might leave some residual impact that could stand in my way of achieving my biggest dream: to become a mother of many children.

Since that day, I lost count of how many home pregnancy tests we bought.

Previously, when I didn't feel ready to have a baby, I never had any trouble expecting my period. It was always very regular and could sense, a week earlier, that it was about to come, due to small changes in my body. But for almost a whole year I couldn't see those signs, even though they were there. It was like my mind kept tricking me, making me ignore those familiar changes. I guess it was because I wanted so much to be pregnant that I made a fool of myself.

I would buy home pregnancy tests and use them despite the fact that my period wasn't late. I just ignored one of those familiar body signs and convinced myself that its supposed absence had to do with an expected pregnancy. But the test would say negative. Then I would blame this undesirable news on the time I took the test or on what I had drunk the night before. So, I would take another one. Then reality would finally hit me and I would stay in peace until the next month, when my period was about to come and I would go over everything again and again.

 I used to buy tests and keep them in my drawer so I didn't have to rush to the store whenever I needed one. It didn't take much until I realized that my dream had become an ideal fantasy. I would worship imaginary children I had not even had, and plan their lives ahead of time, like what they would wear, which languages they would learn at home, or which sports they would practise. Those poor kids were not even conceived and I was already making decisions on their behalf. Thanks to God, I regained my senses before I got into chronic depression or some condition like that. Every time I took a test and saw a "no," it was truly painful to go through this too-familiar cycle: one week of hope and happiness followed by a week of despair and frustration. In the summer of 2012, Frank and I were about to move into our new house. We had so much to do, I thought it would be better to stop trying so hard to conceive a child and instead, let it occur naturally. I decided that I would no longer let a cycle of joy and despair fool me again. I knew

I had to take control of my mind and my thinking. I promised myself that I would never again buy a home pregnancy test unless my period was at least two days late.

To help me in my new task and as a release from the stress of our recent move, Frank suggested that we go camping for a week at our favourite campground by a lake. I loved the idea. Indeed, we had a truly relaxing time and a lot of fun together. Everything was going well until the day we were coming back from camping. We stopped at a coffee house to have breakfast before we planned to head over to Frank's parents.

A message arrived on Frank's cell phone. It came from one of his relatives, whom I will name Elle, and had nothing written on it—just an image of something that Frank couldn't recognize at first. So, he handed the phone over to me, expecting that I could explain to him what it was all about. When I put my eyes on it, I fainted. I had to sit down. Right away, I started to feel huge cramps and my period suddenly arrived, even though it wasn't expected. Frank's relative had chosen to share her joy in a form that she never imagined would be the most painful and humiliating way for us. She sent us a picture of her home pregnancy test with two red lines in it: positive. She was pregnant.

It was the same image that Frank and I had always expected to see, every time I took a test in the past year. I felt devastated.

Once, a friend told me that the enemy uses the people closest to us to hurt us; otherwise, the impact of the resulting suffering would not last long. When we are hurt by someone we have to live around, we will struggle a lot more to love and forgive them, as Jesus has asked us to do.

I'm telling you this because that is exactly what happened to me. This relative of Frank's was very close to us. Since she knew how long we'd been trying to have a baby, I thought she could have taken a different approach to let us know about her pregnancy.
I'm not saying that she wasn't allowed to be happy, to celebrate, and share the news with her family and friends. And I'm not saying that she did this on purpose to hurt us. I do believe, however, that she could have been a lot more sensitive.

Little by little, without noticing, I developed a huge resentment towards her. When I realized what was going on, it was already too late. The situation was completely out of control: I could not stand to even hear her name, let alone see her. But I couldn't avoid some family events. To make things worse, she couldn't avoid talking to me about her morning sickness and how awful she was feeling during her first months of pregnancy. Every time we met, she was always complaining. Many times she told us that being pregnant was almost like dying: it was too painful and beyond control.

A few weeks before she made that horrible comment for the first time, Frank and I had got some unwanted news from our fertility doctor while seated in his office. Fiftyish, thin, and stern, he seemed cold and aloof when speaking to us.

"I'm sorry, but you have a very slim chance of conceiving a child on your own," he told us. "If you really want to be parents some day, you'll need to go through *in vitro* fertilization."

According to the doctor, the reason why we didn't have a baby related to the shape and size of Frank's sperm. He called it "abnormal sperm morphology," which means that misshapen sperm or other defects might affect the sperms' ability to reach and penetrate an egg. He told us that in the sample Frank had provided to the laboratory, his semen analysis had very good volume, vitality, and motility, but none of the sperm had a good morphology.

"That doesn't mean that he is infertile," he reassured us. "He can still father a child, but it may take longer than other couples."

Neither Frank nor I believed this was true. We both remained quiet, paying attention to every word the doctor said. "Having to wait a little longer didn't sound like that big of a problem." I thought.

"There's something else I need to tell you," the doctor added.

Alarmed, we both moved closer to him in our seats.

"You don't have a lot of time. The ovarian reserve test that we did for Sabrina indicates that she is closer to menopause than other women her age." I was thirty-one.

"That's why I recommend that you consider using assisted reproductive technology to conceive a baby." The doctor explained various options to Frank and me as we both sat there, stunned. He wanted us to book the *in vitro* appointment right away, without giving us time to process this news.

Frank and I refused to believe that *in vitro* was our only option. When we left the doctor's office, we even laughed at our supposed infertility. "At least we don't have to spend money with birth control," we joked.

Can you imagine how hard it was for me to hear our relative say something like "I'm dying" just because she had to get up from the couch to throw up again? I was willing to give an arm and a leg to be in her situation. She had no idea how those words sounded in my mind. Here's an example of how I heard her comments: "I am so ungrateful that I can bear a child without having to go through the most embarrassing kind of medical exams" and "I don't appreciate that I never had to hear my doctor saying that it is almost impossible for me and my husband to conceive" and something like "I'm so unhappy that I didn't have to try for almost two years and still not know how much longer I will have to wait to get pregnant."

I know this sounds truly bitter, but that is exactly how I define myself during that time. I knew God wasn't pleased with me nursing these feelings. Besides, I had learned that we must practise forgiveness. In my understanding, prayers and readings will help soften our hearts but only the act of kindness, sacrificing ourselves and our feelings to love the unlovable, can really heal us. Wasn't that what Jesus had taught us on the cross? He took action and walked towards the supreme sacrifice. By doing that, He freed us all from our sins.

Frank's relative didn't know about my feelings or our visit to the doctor, but it was clear that I wasn't interested in her awful stories about how horrible it was to be pregnant. I was determined to obey God and love her; I truly wanted to be at peace with her and with myself. So, I thought we could start by spending some time together. I suggested an afternoon of shopping. Even though we would be shopping for the baby, I thought nothing could be better than that to encourage two women to bond.

I confess I wasn't ready for what was to come. On Easter Friday 2013, we were approaching the day on which we had both agreed to go shopping. While visiting us in our house, Elle realized that she had forgotten to bring the dessert she had made. So, she invited me to go with her to pick it up at her house.

"Are you sure about going out with me to buy baby clothes?" she asked me as we were driving in her car. Before I had time to respond, she continued.

"I'm only asking because I know that you and Frank have been trying to conceive for a long time without success. It sure looks like one or both of you must have some kind of problem, don't you think? I just thought it might be too painful for you to help buy things for my baby when you can't buy for a baby of your own."

I wanted to jump out of the car through the window. For the first time in my life, I couldn't stand up for myself. I was mute. I had no answer. I just wanted to go home and cry. But I put on a brave front.

"Look, I would love to go shopping," I said. "We're not having problems and we'll have a baby when it's the right time."

But I ended up cancelling the next morning, I felt so mad and hurt, I couldn't bear seeing her face.

Elle had caught me off guard. I was already feeling off-kilter that Easter anyway. This significant Christian event is all about Jesus, his death, and resurrection, yet only Frank and I were believers in his family; everybody else was celebrating the Easter egg hunt. As I sat there quietly in her car, I couldn't think of anything except the pain that Jesus went through on the cross. Somehow, I could relate the pain in my Soul to the pain He suffered. Through embarrassment and betrayal, He, too, stood there quietly, praying to God for his ordeal to be over. In my heart, I felt the Holy Spirit reminding me that on Easter Sunday, Jesus was raised from the dead and brought to a place of honour and glory. These unspoken words filled my Soul with hope; in them, I found strength to keep my head up until I could finally get out of this woman's car and return to my home.

A month later, her baby was born; the cutest one I had ever seen. But it took me about two or three months until I could finally let go of my anger towards his mother and hold him in my arms.

And that made me feel good. It made me feel God; he was inside me.

Chapter 22

In God's Basket

"You are worthy, O Lord, To receive glory and honor and power; For You created all things, And by Your will they exist and were created."

Revelation 4:11 (NKJV)

ONE YEAR WENT BY and Frank and I decided it was time to try the *in vitro* fertilization. Our physician sent us to a different specialist at a new fertilization clinic. According to him, it was very good and staff were kind with patients. He also told us that someone from his office would call to book an appointment with the fertility clinic on our behalf, but I didn't want to wait. As soon as we left his office, I called the clinic myself.

It was the first week of May 2014. In a few days, it would be exactly three years since we had been trying to conceive. However, since the doctor's schedule was extremely busy, the first appointment I could get was not until the end of August. Even though we were four months away from our first visit with that new doctor, her assistant immediately emailed us a list of medical exams for Frank and I to take. We were supposed to be getting ready during the waiting time prior to the appointment date.

But we never got them done. Suddenly, all that excitement and anticipation that I had had was gone. Previously, I couldn't wait for a call from the fertility doctor's office; now, I just routinely called them myself. My heart was filled with doubt. As much as I wanted to be a mother, deep inside my heart I didn't feel that *in vitro* was the right thing for us to do. I had no peace. How do I explain to Frank something like that? How could I tell him that I was ready to give up on what seemed our only chance to have a baby? Was I giving up too easily on a dream?

Let me share some thoughts that I have about God and assisted reproductive technology (ART), based only on my personal experience and feelings. I'm not against IVF (*in vitro* fertilization). But I only agree with it if the husband and wife are the only two people involved in the process of providing the sperm and eggs. I did not want to use a surrogate male as a sperm donor. I want to have a child with the man I chose to be my husband; I want to look to my baby and see the mix of both of us. If my husband cannot be the father, I cannot be the mother.

In addition to that, I think that the couple should ensure that the number of eggs fertilized is the same amount that will be implanted. In other words, if three eggs are fertilized and one is implanted, the couple should go back and implant all the remaining eggs. Or ask to have only one egg fertilized. I don't understand couples who pray to have at least one egg fertilized, then they get three; they use one and put the rest in the garbage. We're talking about ending the life of a human being . . . I believe that babies are a gift from God; they are not a goal to pursue or achieve or an object for sale. In my view, if my desire to have a baby is so strong that I agree to a sperm/egg donor, or to someone else carrying my baby in her womb, or to fertilizing the most number of eggs possible so that my chances of becoming pregnant can be maximized, and once I get what I want I discard the rest of the eggs, it's because I never truly wanted to bring life into the world. Instead, I just wanted to fulfill a quest.

.

I also believe in the power of a prayer. I had my prayers answered countless times, so I know that we can change many circumstances by using only a prayer. I even read a book about a woman who was told that her husband could never father a child. After digging into God's Word and praying constantly, she became pregnant with twins with no treatment. But there were also many times where no matter how much I prayed, things didn't happen the way that I wanted. And this was one of those times. Since the day we left the doctor's office, when we got the results from our tests, I've been praying for a miracle.

Once, Frank and I met a man who told us that he and his wife had spent a fortune trying to conceive through IVF. They had the best doctors, the best treatment yet, they still couldn't give birth to a baby. I believe that God, and only God, is the one who breathes life into our bodies. A child brought into this world, either by natural or assisted ways, is blessed by God and is part of His plan for the world, a plan laid out way before we were all created.

It felt like I wasn't trusting in God's power to do the impossible. I was afraid that I was, again, being impulsive and impatient. I didn't want to interfere with God's plans for our lives. There was a reason why Frank and I had to go through all of this. If I truly believed that He is omniscient, who else would know what was best for us?

That period of waiting and wondering and not knowing was definitely the hardest time of my life. I knew that we wanted so much to be parents, but more than that, I wanted God's will above our own. My flesh and my soul were in constant battle. I wanted to do the treatment and try to have babies, but every time I thought about calling the laboratory and booking the exams, I felt a strange mixture of resistance and dread deep in my core. The sensation is hard to explain, but it was similar to what we usually feel when we know we are doing something we aren't supposed to do.

I decided that I would rely on Frank's opinion. "Let him decide," I told myself. But I lied to myself that I was being considerate in consulting him, since we were married and he is the head of our family. I was really just passing the ball to him. (We learned, with time, that the two of us are already one family; children are people we add to the family we formed when we exchanged our vows). I was ready to accept whatever he decided we should do. Because the doctor's appointment was months ahead, I didn't need to rush to have that conversation with him. I had time to pray a little more and to review my thoughts and feelings.

Then, Frank had a dream. He dreamt that he was at the gym where he works, spotting (assisting for safety) a little girl while she was trying to reach for the horizontal bar, also known as the high bar. (This could not happen in real life for two reasons: first, because he doesn't train girls, and second, because the high bar is used only by male gymnasts.) But in his dream, as soon as the little girl gripped the bar, she looked down and with a sweet voice, said to him: "I love you." Frank was so emotional when he told me that. He knew it was more than just a dream—he knew it was a promise.

I felt so horrible. How could I say to the man I love that I wasn't willing to take our only chance (according to the doctors) to see that dream come to pass? One Sunday, while I was at church, the senior pastor announced that his youngest son and wife were having a baby. Another couple, who had been trying for seven years, finally got the good news that they were expecting after they had already given up hope. The pastor finished the announcement by saying that we should never lose hope because there is a time for everything, and that God is always in control.

Hearing that made me wonder if I should agree with Frank, if he wanted me to try the *in vitro*, or try to persuade him not to do it. I was extremely confused. I truly thought that I needed an answer, so I bowed my head and prayed, asking for a sign. At the end of the service, I wanted to ask the pastor's wife to pray with me. I thought that perhaps during our prayer, God could use her to give me a word that would answer my previous question. I wanted Him to tell me if the *in vitro* treatment was something he had planned for us or if the weird feeling I had about it had to do with Him not approving my decision.

But right after I had that thought, another one took hold of me, followed by an overwhelming feeling of God's presence. I heard myself whispering: "If God really wanted to send me a message, He could use anything or anyone to give me the word I needed. It did not necessarily have to come from my pastor's wife to be trustworthy." So, I left the church and went with Frank to his parents' house for lunch as a family. I didn't talk to anyone about my first or second thought. The day went by very fast. We had a lot of fun together, so much so that I completely forgot what had happened that morning at church.

Then my mom called me. I was a little concerned when I recognized her caller ID in my cell phone. She was calling from her home phone (we normally use Skype to communicate) and it was late in Brazil. She told me she had just arrived from church (the service there usually starts at 7:00 p.m.), and she had a message for me. My mom told me that when she was leaving the church, the priest came out to talk to her, asking how Frank and I were doing. Although we had never met him, my mother often talked about us to him. But she had never told him that I wanted to have a baby or that I was wondering if I should pursue the *in vitro* option. I had never even told her that I was having troubles conceiving.

The priest asked her to remind me about the people in the Bible who were healed by faith. When she told me that, I almost passed out. So did my mom. I thought of the Bible verse *"And He said to him, 'Arise, go your way. Your faith has made you well'."* (Luke 17:19 (NKJV)). Since my mom didn't understand why the priest had said that, she was calling to find out the reason. She wanted to talk to me right away, to check up on me. After all, she was concerned.

"I'm shocked," I told her. "I've come to realize how amazing God's ways are. He uses ordinary people to do extraordinary things. I had a question for God and wanted to talk to the pastor's wife this morning because I thought she had such vast experience after walking with God for so many years. And yet, to my surprise, He used you to give me the answer I was looking for. I can't believe this!"

"What?" asked my mother.

"This morning, I prayed and asked God for guidance. And it came the same day." That was all I could tell her. I wasn't ready to give more details about our situation. But I had made my decision. I couldn't tell her that I was happy with it, but after what I had just heard, I was completely sure about what to do next. I had to talk to Frank. I needed to find a way to let him know that I wanted to cancel the fertility doctor's appointment. So, I began to pray for wisdom, asking the Holy Spirit to give me the right words and show me when the best moment would be.

Again, something incredible occurred. On another Sunday, Frank was driving us back from church to our house when he started to share with me his thoughts about our dream to become parents.

"Sweetheart, you know that I will always be by your side and support you, no matter what you decide to do," he said, glancing over at me as he drove. Then he added: "But if you want my honest opinion, I think we should place our wish in God's basket."

Wow! Those were life-giving words.

"I feel exactly the same way," I told Frank. "I was too afraid to tell you that I had second thoughts about the *in vitro* procedure and didn't want to move forward with it."

We both hugged. I gazed into Frank's beautiful blue eyes.

"I thank God for putting you in my life," I told him. "I couldn't be happier than I am right now, with kids or without them; I'm the most blessed woman in the world because I have you."

I knew the significance of "God's basket" because of a cute movie we had watched at home the night before called *Christmas Angel*. In this story, a girl wanted to help her family and entire neighbourhood by placing a wish jar in front of her house. People around her would write down their deepest secret wishes on a piece of paper and place it in the jar. This same girl had a friend whom she thought was an angel. This friend helped her to read and separate the wishes into different baskets: one for impossible things, like getting an A+ without studying, one for possible things, like a new bicycle, and one for God. In this last basket, they put in things they couldn't do but were in accordance with God's word; they could pray about them and let God do the work.

The movie seeks to explore the boundaries between things within our control, over which we have power and should do, as godly people, to help others, and things that only God has control over. Many times, we humans, thinking we are little gods, try to do these only-God-can-do things in our own way. This sometimes results in issues that are a lot bigger than the original problem.

I want to make sure you understand that I'm not saying that God doesn't approve of assisted reproduction. But I truly believe that He gave us the Holy Spirit to guide us through this life and to show us which path we should take. I've learned that if I can't identify His fruits in my decisions, it is probably because I'm doing the opposite of what the Spirit wants. As the Bible says: *"But the fruit of the Spirit is love, joy, peace, long-suffering, kindness, goodness, faithfulness, gentleness, self-control. Against such there is no law"* (Galatians 5:22-23 (NKJV)).

Frank and I believed that the Spirit of God was leading us to put our wish into His basket, to keep praying, and to wait patiently for His will to be done in our lives. In the Bible's words: *"If we live in the Spirit, let us also walk in the Spirit"* (Galatians 5:25 (NKJV)).

We don't know what God has planned. Frank and I have no idea if we will find ourselves expecting, unexpectedly, or if we will be led to adoption. Perhaps we will always be a family of two. But one thing we know for sure: so far, everything God planned for us was better and greater then we could have ever expected. And we can't wait to see what the future holds.

Chapter 23

Still Waiting, but Beating Some Odds

"Those who go down to the sea in ships, Who do business on great waters, They see the works of the Lord, And His wonders in the deep."

Psalm 107:23-24 (NKJV)

I LOVE TO SPEND TIME in my garden. It isn't a large one, but a couple of tall, bushy emerald cedar trees serve as a hedge. Along this hedge, I have planted some flowering shrubs (snow-in-summer) with dark green leaves and little white flowers that smell like honey. I've also planted pink azaleas, an Australian mint bush, and some pink and red *Rio dipladenias*: tropical flowers that thrive all season long. Every day, small visitors come by: bees, birds, and butterflies. The birds love to bathe in our water fountain, then they go and groom themselves under the leaves of the two hydrangea trees that I'm growing in large pots or the banana tree. We bought the latter to put beside our outdoor shower, just to add a tropical resort flavour to it. Around our gazebo we have a lot of hanging baskets filled with red, blue, yellow, orange, and pink petunias. In a raised bed, we are growing the sweetest tomatoes I have ever tasted, strawberries, all kind of lettuces, kale, and spices like mint, cilantro, and basil.

Some people say that gardening is a relaxing activity, and I truly agree with them. It makes me really happy. I even read somewhere that many doctors and psychologists are now suggesting gardening projects for patients who suffer from stress, depression, and dementia.

A beautiful and healthy garden requires a lot of work. It is not just about planting seeds in good soil with enough sunlight and water. We have to keep it up by pulling weeds, fertilizing the soil, watching that bugs don't damage the plants, pruning, and cleaning up in the fall. Phew, just the thought of it makes me sweat. But I still love it. For me, it's a way to connect to God. It's a daily lesson, a reminder that He has a perfect plan and a perfect timing for everything. Like the Bible says: *"To everything there is a season, a time for every purpose under heaven: A time to be born, and a time to die; A time to plant, and a time to pluck what is planted"* (Ecclesiastes 3–1:2 (NKJV)).

I've planted seeds that never sprouted. I planted others, expecting them to bloom in the summer, and they happened to bloom a season earlier. I've learned that it doesn't matter how good the seed, soil or fertilizer I choose is; the plant will grow only when, and if, God allows it to grow.

My garden is real, but I can also use it as a metaphor for my personal life. Frank and I made a decision to trust God and His best interests, which implied that we should be patient. As I've said before, patience was never my forte, and it's not Frank's best asset either. But it is a skill we've both gained over the past few years. It has helped me care for both my garden and my heart. So, here is a friendly suggestion: If you have a garden or a dream, do the best you possibly can, then leave up to God what you cannot do. After that, it's all about waiting.

You may ask: What to do while I wait? Frank and I both agreed that instead of keeping ourselves focused on what we don't have, we will appreciate more what we do have. We have time, we have each other, and we love doing things together. These are things that couples with kids usually complain they cannot do, such as going to the cinema every week or packing for a last-minute trip or waking up late on Sundays (thanks to God, our church offers a service in the afternoon), or crazy and spontaneous things like driving at 2 a.m. with no destination in mind if one of us does not feel like sleeping.

We thought it would be a good idea to use the time we had, while we are just the two of us, to grow deeper in our faith and relationship with God. We also thought we should use this time to bond, to strengthen our marriage, and have some fun. And that was how I got to travel in first class for the first time. Frank and one of his athletes were selected to represent Canada, in Mexico, at a friendly competition hosted in Acapulco. (Unlike at regular competitions, there is no pressure on athletes to win at these fun and informal invitationals. Instead, the simple premise is "Try your best.") For one week in November 2014, they would be with athletes and coaches from other countries such as Russia, the United States, China, Japan, Romania, Spain, Italy, Ukraine, Colombia, Brazil, Uzbekistan, and Mexico. Keeping the idea that we should enjoy ourselves, we agreed that Frank and I should go together.

Frank's tickets were booked by the Mexican Federation and I had to book my own tickets. Blessed to find seats available on each part of the flight, I managed to rearrange Frank's seating so that we could be side by side for all but one connection, the first-class flight from

Mexico City to Acapulco. Yes, it's true that I got a seat in first class, but I didn't book it or pay for it. It was a gift from God.

When buying my tickets, I even thought about paying a little more for first-class comfort and to have my husband sitting by my side. But when I saw how much it would cost me (the same amount we had budgeted to spend for the whole week), I changed my mind. That didn't stop me from asking God, at the last minute, as we were boarding the airplane, to perform a miracle. And it didn't stop God from answering my prayer.

Our flight attendant was the same woman who helped us board; she had seen Frank and me together the whole time we were waiting to get onto the plane. Once we were in the air, she noticed an empty seat beside Frank in first class. That is when I believe God touched her heart. With a big smile, she leaned over Frank's seat and said three words: "Go get her." Delighted at this opportunity, I readily joined Frank in first class.

Throughout that week in Acapulco, I encountered another situation in which only a miracle could explain the outcome. Born and raised in a coastal neighbourhood, I used to surf in the mornings before heading to work. I missed that a lot. That was why, one morning, while Frank was working, I thought it would not be a problem to go for a swim in the ocean. However, my expertise in the water didn't prevent me from getting caught in a rip tide that seemed a lot stronger and more dangerous than the ones I had faced back in Brazil.

Only when I tried to return to the shore did I notice that I had been caught and carried to a deeper area where my feet couldn't find the ground. Frightened, I did the opposite of what you're supposed to do in situations like that: I tried to swim back to the shore, against the current. Drained of my energy and strength, I began to pray, asking God for help. Still praying, I had a peaceful memory of the times when I had surfing lessons. Somehow, I could hear my old instructor telling me to start paddling parallel to the shore. That was what I did. Minutes later, I stood up and felt the sand under my feet. I looked up and thanked God, one more time, for saving me. What a hair-raising experience!

Yet, our last day in Acapulco was incredible. We were able to join in and enjoy a baby sea turtle release with a group of local eco-tourists. This group of people volunteers to find and collect sea turtle eggs and protect them from being eaten until the baby turtles hatch. Once the little turtles are able to make it to the water, these people enable them to return safely to the wild. Frank and

I were able to hold one of the baby turtles in our hands; it was so tiny, fragile, and extremely cute.

As we watched these little creatures use all their strength to reach the ocean, I couldn't help but think that just as they sense they belong to the sea, even though they were born on land, we all share a sort of feeling that we don't belong to this world. Just like them, all we need is someone, a shepherd, to protect us from predators, until the day we cross the finish line, when we can finally say we are home.

But while we are still here, God gives us little glimpses of the life we will have in heaven. This is something to motivate us, to keep us running towards our goal. I believe these are called miracles: supernatural deeds that cannot be explained. As the Bible says:

Jesus said to her, "id I not say to you that if you would believe you would see the glory of God?" Then they took away the stone from the place where the dead man was lying. And Jesus lifted up His eyes and said, "Father, I thank You that You have heard Me. And I know that You always hear Me, but because of the people who are standing by I said this, that they may believe that You sent Me.» Now when He had said these things, He cried with a loud voice, "Lazarus, come forth!" And he who had died came out bound hand and foot with graveclothes, and his face was wrapped with a cloth. Jesus said to them, "Loose him, and let him go" (John 11:40-44 (NKJV)).

Miracles are always attached to a worthy motive. It's in our limitations that God displays His glory and convinces the world of His existence. In the words of the Bible: *"Then many of the Jews who had come to Mary, and had seen the things Jesus did, believed in Him"* (John 11:45 (NKJV)). I know that raising a man from the grave and gaining a free seat in first class aren't a fair comparison, but I meant to show that the miracle itself doesn't really matter. What it inspires in us—that's the real deal. You may not see dead people walking alive (I mean, beyond movies and TV), but miracles are everywhere. They happen every day of our lives. We just don't see them because we are either too busy or refuse to believe in the existence of their Creator God.

God performs daily miracles. It all starts in the morning, when we open our eyes and realize we were given another day, another chance to try something new. As we go through the day, many other miracles take place. If you take a minute to think of how your entire body works (from healthy cells and organs to blood flowing), perhaps you will agree with me that every breath we take is a miracle.

But if, to believe, you still need a story of a person who was "dead" and came back to life, I'll give you three stories. Each one happened to a close family member. Let's start with my father, Jose Sergio. My father grew up in a family that had a lot of prestige. They were never rich, but he carried the weight of a surname that opened many doors. Seen as his parents' favourite by his siblings, my father was raised without knowing the word "no." He grew into a handsome young man and was able to enjoy certain luxuries in life through his creative use of words as a media writer. A confirmed bohemian, he lived between music, art, and literature and spent his nights drinking, smoking, and gambling but lived drug-free.

Because he had a playful personality, he always had a lot of people around. Every time my dad got into trouble, my grandfather was there to bail him out. My father kept drinking and partying until one day, as he was coming home from an after-party, driving drunk, he suffered an accident that changed his life. He crashed his car, wedging it under a truck that he thought was still moving. My dad's vehicle was totally destroyed and he was caught in the wreckage, pinned under the truck for hours, without help.

By a miracle, a family friend passed the crash site and like any curious onlooker, decided to take a closer look. To his surprise, he recognized my father and managed to alert the family and authorities. The right side of my dad's face was destroyed with many facial bones broken. Numerous plastic surgeries were required to repair his injuries. He had his cheekbones replaced by platinum plates and needed a lot of blood. It took him a long time to get back on the road to recovery. None of his doctors believed he would escape death, but his Catholic family knew God could give him a second chance, and He did. My father not only survived the accident and surgeries but also met my mother. With her, he lived the last days of his life, free from drinking and gambling.

Now let me share with you the miracle that God brought recently into my mother's life. A few months after Frank and I returned from our trip to Acapulco, my mother found out that she had something wrong with her thyroid. The doctors recommended a biopsy to figure out the nature and gravity of her problem. According to her family doctor, my mom had an eighty-per-cent chance of being diagnosed with cancer. We all knew it wasn't good news. Information like that is not easy to digest, especially when it involves the people we love and care about.

My mother is a strong woman and she always believed in God, but her faith was shaken. Even though there was a twenty-per-cent chance that her results were due only to thyroid nodules, which aren't serious, she didn't react very well. Afraid of what she could be facing, the lioness became a little kitten. She became very distant; she would reject my calls and come home from work and lock herself in her bedroom, avoiding having any kind of conversation with me or my siblings. The thought of losing my mother, while she was still so young (only fifty-four), terrified me. But I chose to reject those thoughts and instead, believe that God is the same yesterday, today, and tomorrow. He saved my dad and He would save my mom.

Because my mom wasn't willing to talk, I decided to go to Brazil. I wanted to be there for her, during the biopsy, and stand by her side when she received the result. The exam was fast and painless; we waited seven days for the result. Unlike in Canada, patients in Brazil receive laboratory results in a sealed envelope. Doctors expect them to return to the office with it, still sealed, and once there, the physician opens it and reads the results in their presence. This strong recommendation is meant to avoid any confusion for lay people who might open the envelope on their own; unfamiliar with medical terminology, they wouldn't know the true nature of their condition. Still, many people open the envelope regardless, even though they don't understand what is written there. Therefore, I had to keep my mother's results hidden from her from around 8:00 a.m., when we got them, until her 4:00 p.m. doctor's appointment that same day. I had to make sure she wouldn't open the envelope. But I failed. When we got to the clinic, my mom remembered that one of the results was missing.

"Can you please go and get it for me?" she asked me. I went out right away, but forgot to take the biopsy's results with me. When I realized what I had done, I ran back to where she was, hoping that it wasn't too late. Running as fast as I could, elbowing kids and grandmas to open up a way for me (just kidding), I was forced to stop halfway along the walkway and stare. I watched my mother, who was walking fast towards the clinic, suddenly start jumping into the air. Had she gone crazy with the news?

People around us didn't know what was going on. They probably thought she was insane. But when I saw her jumping, I knew the Lord had answered our prayers. She was jumping for joy. I, too, started to jump like crazy. Isn't that a miracle?

Perhaps you still think it was nothing but luck. Well, here is my third story. My mom had reacted so badly to the scary news, instead of believing right away that she didn't have cancer, because my grandpa, her father, has been fighting bladder cancer for almost ten years. When we found out that he had cancer, it was a shock. He was always very active and seemed so healthy. The doctor said that bladder cancer is highly treatable but can return. Because of its constant recurrence, my grandpa had to go through nine surgery procedures to have tumors removed. Thankfully, he recovered very well after each one.

In December 2014, at age ninety-two, my grandpa suffered an ischemic stroke (a loss of blood flow to the brain, caused by reduced blood pressure, a blood clot or embolism), which almost took him away from us. But once again, our faith and prayers beat the odds. The doctors were amazed with his recovery. He spent only seven days in the intensive care unit and soon after that, he was at home, ready to start his rehabilitation.

My grandfather's name is Pedro Rocha. "Pedro," in Greek, means "rock," and "Rocha" is a Portuguese family name that also means rock. He believes and trusts in God. As I write this book, he is now ninety-three years old. It's no wonder Mr. Rock Rock is so hard to break. He has God on his side.

Chapter 24

The Call of Duty

"Fight the good fight of faith, lay hold on eternal life, to which you were also called and have confessed the good confession in the presence of many witnesses."

1 Timothy 6:12 (NKJV)

IT WAS THE SECOND Sunday of May in 2014. Since Frank and I were looking for a church to call home, some of our friends invited us to attend a service at their local church. For some time, we had both felt, in our hearts, the desire to make a change; at times in our spiritual life, God makes us dissatisfied with where we are to prepare us to go somewhere else. And yet, in many ways, we were so comfortable where we were; people at our existing church were always so friendly and our pastors were great. Besides, Frank is not someone who likes change. I was afraid that while leaving that specific church to look for another, we would end up getting lost along the way. So, we kept postponing it until our senior pastor announced his retirement. Then it became clear for Frank and I that it was the right time to move churches.

While still looking, we thought it was okay to join our friends and check out their church. After all, many places called "a church" are far from what we call The House of the Lord. They may talk about God, Jesus, and the Holy Spirit, but unfortunately, in these places, their view of each person of the divine trinity and what they represent to us is not exactly what the Bible says.

It was Mother's Day. I always get emotional on this day because I long to become a mom and also because my mother is so far away; I must celebrate without her. So, I thought that having our friends by my side would help me keep my tears under control. Theirs was a very nice and small church, which allows the pastor to know everybody by name and to recognize new faces like ours. They were very much aligned with the Bible and we felt welcomed there. Even though we decided to keep searching, I believe that Frank and I were meant to be at that church that day because of the sermon delivered by that young and wise pastor.

"Remember to appreciate both of your parents and care for them," he told us, "not only on special occasions like today but throughout the entire year."

He looked out at the congregation from behind the podium. "And please be mindful, you women who have never been pregnant or have never carried a pregnancy to term. You are not a failure, certainly not in God's eyes. In fact, according to Him, but mostly according to the Bible, you women were created first to be a helper, a companion, not mainly to procreate. You and your role are just right for your husbands."

I remembered what the Bible says:

So Adam gave names to all cattle, to the birds of the air, and to every beast of the field. But for Adam there was not found a helper comparable to him. And the Lord God caused a deep sleep to fall on Adam, and he slept; and He took one of his ribs, and closed up the flesh in its place. Then the rib which the Lord God had taken from man He made into a woman, and He brought her to the man" (Genesis 2:20-22 (NKJV)).

The pastor's words were healing and soothing for me, and I certainly needed to hear them. Many of us, struggling to conceive, tend to believe that we are, somehow, incomplete. That often causes us to feel ashamed and humiliated, as if it were our fault that we cannot bear a child. But deep inside of me, I knew that assisting my husband wasn't my only calling. I'm sure that God wants me to be an excellent companion for Frank, but I also knew that He expected a lot more from me than just taking care, exclusively, of one person for my whole life.

As I grew in my relationship with God, I learned to pay close attention to the unusual dreams that I often had, even though they scared me to death most of the time. Usually, they signified something important that would later help me understand a situation, to identify a good opportunity or prevent me from making a bad decision. I believe that both God and Satan, the enemy, can use these dreams to communicate with us. I learned to distinguish which one had created my weird dream by the message that it brings, by whether it encouraged me to do something good and aligned with the Scriptures or not.

During this time, I had two dreams that I believe came from God. The first one happened a few days before I travelled to Brazil, in March, when we thought my mom could be seriously sick. In that dream, I was a kind of teacher. I was responsible for some kids and we were all together, inside a swimming pool, having some fun. Then, all of a sudden, a war began. We could hear loud noises and saw many balls of fire falling from the sky right above us. Trying to save ourselves, I guided the kids to dive into the bottom of the pool, which was some sort of passage way to a different place. As we did so, we crossed the border of a big field, which was very green and peaceful.

The new land we were in belonged to someone I didn't know. But he kindly allowed everybody to build their own house. Frank was there with me and for me, but for some reason, we no longer lived in the same house. In this new city, nobody lived together under the same roof. We were all living with and for each other, on the same piece of property, just like one big community or commune. After some time, I realized that one of these kids, a girl whom I loved the most, hadn't crossed the border. She stayed behind. I cried, and the pain of losing her was so big that I passed out.

A few hours later, I woke up in my bed with a pain in my chest, feeling the overwhelming weight of losing someone that I love. I understood, immediately, that this was a sign, a message that not everybody I love will go to heaven, when the time comes. This will only happen if they open their hearts to receive the salvation that Jesus offers. Since that day, I have made a list of the names of people that somehow were part of my life and of those who are still present, around me. I started to pray for them and for those that I will probably never meet. I was sure that this was the only thing I needed to do. In my mind, I had that dream because God wanted me to pray for them.

But a week after that, I had the second dream. This one was a lot more disturbing than any dream I had ever had. In this one, a cloud of dust, huge and strong, destroyed everything. People were panicking and running over each other. It didn't even matter if they were running over members of their own family; the only thing they wanted, in that moment, was to find a safe place to spare their own lives. In the midst of that chaotic situation, Frank and I decided we would not run. Instead, we would walk slowly, but make sure that we remained together. We also had a young boy with us.

We walked a lot. People were still in a panic, pushing and pressuring us to walk faster, but we stood strong. We kept moving at a slow pace, holding our hands together firmly. After some time, we saw a door. As we approached it, I heard a loud voice quoting this Biblical verse: *"Ask, and it will be given to you; seek, and you will find; knock, and it will be opened to you"* (Matthew 7:7 (NKJV)). So, we knocked and a man showed up, presenting himself as Jesus. He came downstairs and opened the door, letting Frank and I come in, but not the boy. I don't know why, but he didn't want to let the young boy in.

So, we asked kindly and vehemently, just as we had read and heard in Scripture that we should. But this man didn't answer our prayer. I remember him as very mean; he didn't want to listen.

"I understand that not everything we ask, thinking it is good, is given," I told him, still dreaming, "because only God knows what is really good or not for us. But what we are asking here is for salvation. And according to the Scriptures, everyone who calls on Jesus's name for help should receive forgiveness for their sins and salvation."

In the dream, Frank and I figured out that such a person could not be Jesus. Instead, he was the evil one, pretending to be Him, trying to deceive us to enter that door alone, to save ourselves, and forget the boy. We caught him in a lie because we knew God's word and he wasn't aware we did. We rebuked him and he left.

When I woke up, breathing heavily, I realized the need to know and understand the Word of God, to differentiate what is right from what is not, what is from God and what is from the evil one. Since the dream showed that I was again looking after a child, it made me realize that I had unfinished business. Many years ago, I had made a promise to God, and now it was time to pay on that promise.

Back when I was in Brazil, Vania and the other elders of our church had told me, after many prayers, and after they had laid their hands over my head, that I was called to be an evangelist, to preach the gospel, to announce the Good News and to call others to believe in Jesus and be saved. Over and over, I would hear in my head a still, small voice quoting the passage where Jesus asked Peter three times if he loved Him. Just like Peter did, I denied Jesus before I became a Christian. In my case, it was two times, not three: when I moved to the same building as Vania and ignored her efforts to talk to me about God's Word, and when Tina talked to me about Him. The Bible says:

So when they had eaten breakfast, Jesus said to Simon Peter, "Simon, son of Jonah, do you love Me more than these?" He said to Him, "Yes, Lord; You know that I love You." He said to him, "Feed My lambs." He said to him again a second time, "Simon, son of Jonah, do you love Me?" He said to Him, "Yes, Lord; You know that I love You." He said to him, "Tend My sheep." He said to him the third time, "Simon, son of Jonah, do you love Me?" Peter was grieved because He said to him the third time, "Do you love Me?" And he said to Him, "Lord, You know all things; You know that I love You." Jesus said to him, "Feed My sheep" (John 21:15-17 (NKJV)).

It was clear to me that just as Peter had done, I, too, should feed His sheep and follow Him, if I really loved Jesus as I said I did. So, for a little while, I did some preaching for the Catholic charismatic renewal movement in my hometown. When I moved to Canada, I was invited once or twice to preach online, using a webcam. But after that, I stopped being active and became a passive Christian.

Even though I ceased to serve, Jesus kept reminding me that my testimony could help many sheep who went missing like me to find their way back to the Good Shepherd. My experiences could be used to help people get to know God and what He is able to do for each of us. The Bible says: *"And other sheep I have which are not of this fold; them also I must bring, and they will hear My voice; and there will be one flock and one shepherd"* (John 10:16 (NKJV)). Through dreams, sweet voices in my head, verses from the Bible, and the testimony of others, God has been using a lot of ways to remind me that I am an evangelist. Therefore, I must share the Gospel.

But the method He used to push me to the edge, which truly made me take a stand, was the preaching of our pastor in our new church. Yes, after some prayer and research, Frank and I found a church that we call home.

Since we decided to stay, we've been called to serve in every service we attend. You might say that every church does the same thing, and I should agree with you, but there is something different about this specific church and their leaders.

To them, our call to serve is more than just a calling—it is a call of duty.

I've found myself with a duty to tell the world that I was created by God to report everything He does and has done for me, my family, and my friends, so that we can show the right path to those who are lost and the way back to those who are weak in faith. The Bible says it best: *"For the gifts and the calling of God are irrevocable"* (Romans 11:29 (NKJV)).

Chapter 25

I Always Had My Head in a Book

"And He commanded us to preach to the people, and to testify that it is He who was ordained by God to be Judge of the living and the dead. To Him all the prophets witness that, through His name, whoever believes in Him will receive remission of sins."

Acts 10:42-43 (NKJV)

I BELIEVE WE ARE ALL called to do something in life. Some people are called to do great things. Others are called to do things in a great way. Both groups of people influence our world with their actions. In the beginning of this book, I mentioned that I always wanted to belong to a group of people who do great things: everybody knows about them and respects them for what they have achieved. But after I became a follower of Christ, I realized that people who do great things, like He did, are the ones doing things for love and not for recognition.

Besides my calling to help my husband and the strong urge to help others get to know God and the Gospel, there was something else I knew I should do. Since I was young, long before I became a follower of Christ, I had this idea of writing a book. But at that time, I was too busy trying to impress my mother. As I grew older, I kept postponing it, with the excuse that I didn't know where to start. After I gave my life to Jesus, the thought that I should write became more frequent. So, I started to gather some old diaries, sticky notes, and little pieces of paper where I had written about my life and my feelings, hoping that I would finally be encouraged to start writing.

But in the same way I knew that I had to stop and write, I was also aware, deep inside of me, that stopping meant a lot more than just dedicating a few hours of my day to it. It meant a sacrifice that I wasn't willing to make; it meant that I should dedicate one hundred percent of my time to the book. In other words, in my view, I had to quit my job.

Reading and writing are one of my passions. My love for reading started early in life, when I was still a little girl and didn't know how to read. It all started with my father, a freelance journalist who used to cover events organized by members of high society in our small town.

Every day, after work, he would bring home the new edition of my favourite comic book and read it all night long to me and my baby sister, until we both fell asleep. If I close my eyes, I can still see him entering the house with a newspaper under his arm and my comics in his hands. I remember being at the door, waiting for his arrival, and jumping into his arms to grab my gift so that I could take a first look before dinner.

After my dad passed away, when I was five, we had to move to a smaller place. I had so many comics that my mom didn't know how to fit them all into our little room, so she gave most of them away. Of course, I was devastated. Trying to ease my sadness, my mother promised to keep the tradition of buying a new one every now and then, and letting me choose the old ones I could keep.

Time went by, and I was soon able to read by myself. I used to read those comics every day, over and over, so much so that later on, I started to tell the stories from memory to my younger sister. Soon enough, I was adding new content to the stories and eventually, I started to create my own. When I learned how to write, I already had my own stories in my mind, so I just had to put them all together on paper. I haven't stopped writing since. In my teens, I started to write journals and poetry. I even wrote a play for the celebration at the end of the school year.

Yes, I love writing. But quitting my job was, by far, one of the most difficult decisions I had to make, mostly because it never made sense to me (not in the beginning, at least). I knew that authors and publishers have to put together a lot of effort until they can finally hold their book in their hands. But in times like today, when the unemployment rate increases every year, leaving a full-time job that offers health benefits, a pension plan, bonuses, and an employee share purchase plan was a little too crazy for me.

So, I ignored the feeling (it was more like an urge) that I needed to quit work. Many times during the past few years, I tried to write the book during my spare time, as almost every writer does. But I had no success. The closest I got to having something worthy in print to share with others was a group of chapters that I wrote in Portuguese—my first attempt to write this book. But with time, I realized that the writing was really plain and without creativity. You could easily feel that my heart wasn't there. So, I decided that instead of quitting my job to write the book, I should forget this whole idea of writing and keep working and enjoying the perks of having a steady income.

But as I said before, writing a book wasn't my idea, but something I was meant to do. So, God kept talking to me, not letting me forget. Believe me, like Jonah, I tried to run away and hide, but thankfully, God never gives up. The Bible says: *Now the word of the Lord came to Jonah the son of Amittai, saying, "Arise, go to Nineveh, that great city, and cry out against it; for their wickedness has come up before Me." But Jonah arose to flee to Tarshish from the presence of the Lord. He went down to Joppa, and found a ship going to Tarshish; so he paid the fare, and went down into it, to go with them to Tarshish from the presence of the Lord* (Jonah 1:1-3 (NKJV)).

Just as God used a whale to persuade Jonah to do what he was called to do, with me it was no different. In Jonah's case, the Bible reads: *"Now the Lord had prepared a great fish to swallow Jonah. And Jonah was in the belly of the fish three days and three nights"* (Jonah 1:17 (NKJV)). Well, I wasn't swallowed by a whale, but He did send an animal to get me to change my mind. I was walking by the Centennial Seawalk in West Vancouver, during my lunch break, admiring the most beautiful sailboats on the water to my right. I was wondering how great it would be to have a cup of coffee, watching the same scenery from one of those million-dollar-view apartments, when the idea of writing a book started to hit me again.

Right away, as a defense mechanism, I asked God how I could ever achieve something like that if I quit working. I just didn't understand why I couldn't do both, work and write. In a split second, a small bird landed right beside me, trying to catch a worm from the grass. I heard that small voice in my heart, quoting me the Bible: *"Look at the birds of the air, for they neither sow nor reap nor gather into barns; yet your heavenly Father feeds them. Are you not of more value than they?"* (Matthew 6:26 (NKJV)).

I still remember me saying out loud: "I get it," minutes before heading back to work and telling my supervisor that I would be leaving the company in two weeks. But I guess my employer liked the work I was doing there because a few days later, I was given a promotion. Even though I realized that I didn't need an expensive apartment, and that God would provide for my real needs, the idea of becoming the owner of a fancy boat looked a lot more attractive than becoming an unemployed writer.

I never said that I wasn't stubborn. . . But I did already say that our Heavenly Father never gives up on us. And he didn't give up on me. One year later, in August 2014, the pastor who wrote the book mentioned in the first pages of this one, which helped me open my heart to receive the Good News, was in Vancouver, preaching in a big event promoted by his ministry. Frank thought it would be a great birthday gift to buy tickets so that we could both attend.

The event was great with a lot of worshipping, prayers, testimonies, and an encouraging message. At the end of the service, we had the opportunity to meet and shake hands with the pastor outside the auditorium. I know it will sound silly, but in that moment, when I was shaking his hand, I realized that I should write this book, no matter what kind of sacrifice I had to make. Standing in front of me was the man who had led me to Jesus, a man made of flesh and bones, just like you and me. The only difference between that man and I was that he decided to walk towards his dreams. He didn't fear criticism and he believed that God would help him do the work he was called to do, as He did.

On our way home, Frank motivated me to quit my job.

"Remember all those times when you weren't ashamed to get up alone at church, to worship God, dancing and singing, sometimes out of tune?" he asked me.

"Was I really that bad?" I asked, laughing.

"Well, at those times, when I looked at you, I saw someone who wasn't afraid of failing. For you, while in the presence of God, nothing else seemed to matter."

"You're right. That's truly how I felt."

"Well, if you could pour that love into your writing, I'm sure that God will meet you in your limitations and bring your dream to pass."

I stared at Frank, amazed at his clarity, love, and support for me. And that was how I got the courage to deliver my resignation letter to my supervisor. One month later, I had no job and no idea of what I should write about. I was sure that I had testimony to give. I needed to share the story of my life, how God took me out of the darkness, and what it meant to me and my family when He brought me to the light. But I didn't know how to write that down in the form of a book. Besides that, I also had the fear that people would not receive the message I had to share because of my lack of experience both as a writer and as an evangelist.

Time was going by fast, which made me really nervous. Thinking that it would take me a lot more than just three months to write the book, as I had originally planned, I ended up applying for a few jobs.

I worried that my savings wouldn't be enough to keep up with the lifestyle we were used to, but every time

I was invited for an interview, I would feel really bad in the presence of the interviewer, like I wasn't doing something right. I would then apologize and ask to have my application withdrawn. Desperate for help, I started fasting and praying every morning for a few hours. I would read the Bible, meditate on the message, and write down what I understood from it. At all times, throughout the day, I would ask God to show me a way.

It didn't take long before words began to pop into my mind. They would come in English, which scared me at first. It would have been a lot easier for me to write this book in Portuguese, but God made clear to me, during my morning prayers, that I live in Canada, where French and English are the official languages. There is nothing more respectful than addressing a culture in its own language.

I learned in school that if I wanted to be heard, I must make myself understood. And if someone didn't understand what I was trying to say, it was probably because I had failed to communicate.

As I advanced in writing the chapters, unexpected things started to happen, both good and bad. For example, a cheque arrived in my name, ready to be cashed out, from a retirement account that my previous employer had opened and deposited on my behalf. I knew that after working for that company for two consecutive years, we were eligible to have a retirement plan, but I had no idea that I could cash the money, even though I had resigned. That money was a great help.

One night, while Frank was driving home from work, a silver minivan hit the left side of our car, then took off. Thanks to God, nothing happened to Frank. We had insurance, but would not have been able to pay the deductible if wasn't for that extra money. Similarly, a few weeks before the accident, we would not have been able to buy a new set of tires when a massive piece of metal, left on the road, ripped one of our tires.

One of the good things was receiving a delivery notice at my door, during Christmas, from my favorite coffee shop. Since I'm from Brazil, where coffee is king, you have the perfect idea of how much I enjoy sipping a good shot of espresso during the day. While previously working, I never minded paying a little extra for a better coffee taste. But a couple of months after I left my job, Frank and I came to our senses: specialty coffee was a luxury that we needed to cut out of our budget. I tried to persuade Frank to do otherwise, with pleas like "but I really like the taste," but he was right. I agreed that we should stop purchasing those coffee capsules and start making our own coffee with coffee beans, as most people do.

I guess God saw how much I liked those capsules and wanted me to have some for Christmas. The delivery notice at my door was for a box containing two weeks of the most amazing coffee taste, all for free. You might ask: Free coffee, just like that? Yes, I readily answer, just like that. All because God can! (Later, I found out that Nespresso sent a "Christmas treat" to its loyal customers.) Just like how I became a Canadian citizen a lot earlier than we expected. Everybody was amazed that it all happened so fast.

Six years ago, while still in Brazil, working in a bank for the government, I was back at university to pursue a career as an English teacher because I was looking for a change. I've already told you that. It never crossed my mind that one day, I would be married to a great man (a follower of Christ), living in Canada, and writing a book about my life story, let alone taking the oath of citizenship two months before my in-laws, who had lived in Canada for fifteen years.

The crazy thing about this is that I applied for my citizenship status in February 2014, one month *after* they had applied for theirs. I couldn't apply at the same time they did because I hadn't been living in Canada long enough. A minimum of 1,095 days (three years) is required, after you become a permanent resident, before you can send in your application. I will never forget the day after my citizenship ceremony. My in-laws, Frank, and I were sitting around the table, having dinner, and Frank's dad asked me, "Who do you know higher up who speeded up the process for you?"

"God!" I answered, in a heartbeat, pointing to heaven and still with some food left in my mouth. As the Bible says: *"All Your works shall praise You, O Lord, And Your saints shall bless You. They shall speak of the glory of Your kingdom, And talk of Your power, To make known to the sons of men His mighty acts, And the glorious majesty of His kingdom"* (Psalm 145:10-12 (NKJV)).

Chapter 26

A Letter from Me to You

"That which was from the beginning, which we have heard, which we have seen with our eyes, which we have looked upon, and our hands have handled, concerning the Word of life— the life was manifested, and we have seen, and bear witness, and declare to you that eternal life which was with the Father and was manifested to us—that which we have seen and heard we declare to you, that you also may have fellowship with us; and truly our fellowship is with the Father and with His Son Jesus Christ. And these things we write to you that your joy may be full."

1 John 1:1-4 (NKJV)

DEAR FRIEND,

Please, allow me to call you a friend.

As you can see, this book is not about me, although I did use the story of my life as an illustration. This is a book about redemption; in other words, it is about God and his immeasurable Love for us.

I've been trying to write to you for the past five years. I wanted to share some wisdom that I accumulated throughout my journey, including my old life, all of my mistakes, all of the pain I went through, and the pain that I caused the people I met.

When I was young, and my mother came to me with advice, I would argue with her and tell her that our stories were different and that I needed to learn from my own experiences. Only now can I see how foolish that was. I wish that I had listened to her. It would have saved me from many troubles and much hurt. I also wish that I had given my life to Jesus when I first had the opportunity, when I lived in the same building as my friend Vania.

I don't know about you, but I was really stubborn. To be honest, I'm still working on that. Many times, I catch myself trying to bargain with Our Heavenly Father, trying to fit my will into His, when I know I should be fitting His will into mine. Many were the times when I asked God to take me out of a bad situation that I had caused only because I failed to listen to Him, because I ignored His teachings.

If I had listened to my mom when she said Tom was too old for me or when she forbade us from seeing each other or if I had respected her authority instead of disobeying her, my story would have been a lot different. The Bible says: *"Children, obey your parents in the Lord, for this is right. 'Honour your father and mother,' which is the first commandment with promise: 'that it may be well with you and you may live long on the earth'"* (Ephesians 6:1-3 (NKJV)).

But if I knew that the only way for me to surrender my life to Jesus was by going through all the struggles I did, I would not have taken away one single minute of that pain. If I could go back in time, knowing this was the only way I could stand where I am today, the only way I would learn everything I know (still a lot to learn), or meet the people I have met, I would do it all again. *It was worth it!* I'm not proud of the wrong things I've done. For that, I already asked God, myself, and others for forgiveness. I know that God forgave me through Christ, when I accepted Him in my life as my Lord and Saviour. After that, I learned how to forgive myself and humbly approach others, asking them to pardon me.

See, I wasn't any smarter than you. I just chose to be free from guilt and shame, rather than living in fear and regret.

I hope this book can help you to learn from my personal experience, to make the right decision. If you are facing a similar quandary today, either you are ignoring advice from your loved ones and/or from God. I beg you, please, don't fool yourself with that same thought of "I want to learn from my own mistakes."

If you failed to listen and obey, like I did, I hope this book can help you understand that it doesn't matter what kind of trouble you are in today, this is not the end. *There is a way out!*

I invite you to try the Love of Christ. I know it seems to be a hard thing to do. I also know that you're probably wondering about the changes you will have to make to follow His lead. I know because I've been in your shoes. And because I've been there, I can assure you that you don't have to make any change in your life to receive His Love. It's a gift, given to all of us, for free. There are absolutely no conditions attached to His offer.

Frank and I, together with many other believers, left our old selves behind once we started to follow Jesus. But the changes you've read about happened only because once we opened our hearts to receive Jesus's offer, we realized that there is nothing greater than His Love for us.

Let me give you an illustration. We all know that the smartest thing to do when people owe money is to cut their expenses and perhaps downsize their car and even house to pay off that debt. But for people who give much importance to material things and don't care about accumulating debts, offering such a logical solution is a waste of time. It will never work. Those people will never be motivated to lose what they value the most.

To get them to agree to change their ways, stop spending money, start paying bills, and caring for the future, you must offer something greater than the pleasure that having those things can offer them. The same happens in every other area of our lives: only a greater Love can motivate us to leave something we love behind.

So, I invite you, again, to try the Love of Christ. Don't worry if doesn't make sense to the people you hang out with. It probably didn't make sense to you either when I said I quit my job to write this book. But if you just open your heart to receive it, like I did, you, too, will see that things that sometimes make no sense to others feel just right to us.

Once you know, deep in your heart, that the Maker of the universe and of everything in it approves of what you are doing, you feel confident enough to go against the flow. Would you be willing to accept this truth? The Bible says:

For we ourselves were also once foolish, disobedient, deceived, serving various lusts and pleasures, living in malice and envy, hateful and hating one another. But when the kindness and the love of God our Saviour toward man appeared, not by works of righteousness which we have done, but according to His mercy He saved us, through the washing of regeneration and renewing of the Holy Spirit, whom He poured out on us abundantly through Jesus Christ our Saviour, that having been justified by His grace we should become heirs according to the hope of eternal life (Titus 3:3-7 (NKJV)).

To you who have already accepted Jesus as your Lord, but for some reason feel you've been disconnected from Him, I invite you to come back. Remember: We are all a work-in-progress.

Sometimes, I feel I'm like a baby trying to walk in Jesus's steps, as I lose my balance and fall. But then He runs in my direction and, with much love and mercy, lifts me up and helps me find my balance, over and over again.

Dear friend, Christ is extending His hands right now to you too. Would you let Him help you get up? As the Bible says: *"For we do not have a High Priest who cannot sympathize with our weaknesses, but was in all points tempted as we are, yet without sin. Let us therefore come boldly to the throne of grace that we may obtain mercy and find grace to help in time of need"* (Hebrews 4:15-16 (NKJV)).

As we approach the end of this book, I would like to thank you for choosing to spend your precious time with me. I really appreciate that. Before I go, I would like to pray for you.

"Father,

"Thank you for the life of my friends who are reading this book right now. For all that they are, and for all that they are becoming. If they are reading this book, it is because they are looking to learn more from You.

"Lord, it isn't easy to live in this world without getting lost. Many people refuse to be part of Your family because they lack in knowledge of Your love for them. There are also people that know about You, but don't want to belong to Your family because they don't want to get rid of their sinful nature.

"I'm not here to judge, because I myself fall short before You. But I'm humbly asking You to send the Holy Spirit to fill their lives with Your presence, so they can understand that You, and only You, are what they are looking for.

"The enemy will try to stop them, will put fear in their hearts and doubts in their souls. People around them will say they have lost their minds. They will ask them to stop and get back to their 'normal' lives.

"These people will use every little fall to prove that my friends are doing wrong by following You. I pray that You will empower them to shake off fear and criticism from their hearts and keep them safe so they can move forward towards Your Kingdom.

"Help them, God, to keep their eyes always focused on what really matters. Let them know that there is no secret. We need Jesus, to reach out for Your love. As it is written in Your word, He is the way. Through Him, we can live a life of abundant love. In the words of the Bible: *"Jesus said to him, 'I am the way, the truth, and the life. No one comes to the Father except through Me'"* (John 14:6 (NKJV)).

"Please, when the time comes when we wrongly think You have forgotten us, when the trials hit our core and shake our faith, send them a sign, a friend, a song, a word, something to remind them that You are with them and for them, that You will help them overcome evil. Please, let them be reminded that You never break your promises and of how much You love them. As the Bible tells us: *"He who does not love does not know God, for God is love. In this the love of God was manifested toward us, that God has sent His only begotten Son into the world, that we might live through Him"* (1 John 4:8-9 (NKJV)).

"Heavenly Father, I finish my prayer by asking You to bless their lives, so that they, too, can testify about

You, in everything they do, at all times. Send the Holy Spirit upon them and baptize them with fire. Keep the flame burning for love, kindness, justice and truth.

"Thank you, Lord."

Epilogue

MY FRIEND, I hope that you enjoyed reading this book as much as I had fun writing it. It wasn't easy to open up and share my life with everyone. But I have a great love for God's children and a huge desire to join the mission and spread His word to all people in the world. As the Bible says: Love overcomes all. To quote a related verse: *"There is no fear in love; but perfect love casts out fear, because fear involves torment. But he who fears has not been made perfect in love"* (1 John 4:18 (NKJV)).

This love empowered me so that I could win the battle against my fear of talking about my past. I could overcome my pain of telling others why I do not have a child.

For the past six months, as I was putting these words together, little by little, I got drawn nearer to God; every day, I could experience a bit more of His healing power.

I honestly hope that this work can help you as much as it has already helped me.

I cannot say goodbye without encouraging you to follow your dreams. Listen: If God placed them in your heart, He will make it happen. Don't let time, people, or your fears talk you out of it. Instead, learn to protect your dreams. Believe, pray, and go for it.

More than anybody else, I know that life is not always like we planned. But I promise you, if you keep your heart open for what God has planned for you, it will turn out better than you could ever expect. Through your journey, please find comfort in the words of Psalm 23, as I have done:

The Lord is my shepherd; I shall not want. He makes me to lie down in green pastures; He leads me beside the still waters. He restores my soul; He leads me in the paths of righteousness For His name's sake. Yea, though I walk through the valley of the shadow of death, I will fear no evil; For You are with me; Your rod and Your staff, they comfort me. You prepare a table before me in the presence of my enemies; You anoint my head with oil; My cup runs over. Surely goodness and mercy shall follow me All the days of my life; And I will dwell in the house of the Lord, Forever (Psalm 23 (NKJV))

I would be happy to hear from you. If you have any questions or comments, please feel free to email me at contact@brinaszabo.com.

Love,

Sabrina

Bibliography

The Holy Bible. New King James Version. Thomas Nelson Inc. Nashville, Tennessee. 1982.

Used by permission. All rights reserved.

Made in the USA
Middletown, DE
06 October 2018